*Contemporary Prayers
for Public Worship*

Contemporary Prayers for Public Worship

by Anthony Coates, John Gregory,
Caryl Micklem, William Sewell, David Stapleton,
Roger Tomes and Brian Wren

edited by Caryl Micklem

SCM PRESS LTD

First published 1967
by SCM Press Ltd
56 Bloomsbury Street London W C 1

Second impression 1967

© SCM Press Ltd 1967

Printed in Great Britain by
Robert Cunningham & Sons Ltd
Alva Scotland

Contents

Part III

PRAYERS FOR THE CHRISTIAN YEAR

Appendix

THE LORD'S PRAYER

Introduction

It is imperative that material for congregational worship should be made more generally available by special publication . . . We would urge all churches to encourage bold and informed experiments in worship and to stimulate co-operation in such action at the local level. We would ask the British Council of Churches to ensure that information about such experiments and relevant material should be made readily available.

It is by those recommendations of the Nottingham Faith and Order Conference of 1964, and by the experimental orders of service which have subsequently appeared in *The Expository Times*, that the compilers of the prayers which follow have been encouraged to offer their work for the consideration of the Church at large. Prepared in the first place for Congregationalist worship, the material will (we realize) be of little direct use to those with fixed liturgies: indirectly, however, we hope that the issues raised by what we have attempted will make this a helpful contribution to the general liturgical conversation. We believe that the question of the use of modern language and thought-forms in prayer no less than in preaching must in the end be faced by those of 'free' and 'liturgical' traditions alike.

So far, remarkably little has been published that exhibits, or furthers, the facing of these questions. Guy Daniel's *The Enemy is Boredom* (Darton, Longman and Todd) includes modern translations of the Collects and Communion Service from the Book of Common Prayer (which is one reason why we have not attempted the Collects here); William Barclay, in *Prayers for the Christian Year* (SCM Press), bases modern prayers upon the Collects; and a few of George MacLeod's modern-language prayers appear in *Four Men and Our Faith* (Iona Community). From the Roman Catholics we have Michel Quoist's *Prayers of Life* (Gill, Dublin), and Hamman's modern translations of prayers from the ancient liturgies in *Early Christian Prayers* (Longmans). Nowhere, as far as we know, is there a collection of original contemporary prayers comprehensive enough to be used as a working manual by ministers of the Free Churches and the Church of Scotland who wish to experiment in this direction.

We mean to encourage on-the-spot experimentation, not to provide a substitute for it. It will often happen, however, that a minister will be able to prepare one 'contemporary' prayer or group of prayers for a service, but not the rest. We hope this book will provide him with material (which he can adapt to his own style), and at the same time stimulate him to extend the range of his own experiments.

Our own chief stimulus has undoubtedly been the publication, and regular use in our own churches, of the *New English Bible*. Once, it was only in the sermon and the notices, if then, that modern language was heard in church. Lessons, prayers and hymns were all solidly archaic, and each was the more readily accepted because of the other two. Since 1961, this bloc has been breached. Although official Anglican revisers have so far been conservative, it has begun to seem plainly incongruous that the people who have just listened to the ancient gospel record in the language of their own time should be asked to make their personal, up-to-date response to the gospel in the language of the day before yesterday. In this situation, modernization of the language of public prayer is the obvious starting-point. In the case of hymns, which cannot be modernized but only replaced, the incongruity is bound to persist for some years yet – until the volume of contemporary writing of words to be sung, be they hymns or carols or more like folk-song, increases comparably with the production of modern tunes.

This may be expected to happen now that the changing situation is beginning to demand it. Already the English translation of the Psalms made by The Grail (England) for singing to the tunes of Gelineau has taken things a long step further on. Many congregations sing these versions, and many more ministers use them in leading worship, if not directly then indirectly in the preparation of their own prayers. The parts of the service still in seventeenth-century language begin to look like islands in a rising tide – especially when the Old Testament lesson is from Moffatt or from J. B. Phillips's *Four Prophets*. Once the *New English Bible* is complete, and the Old

Testament grandeur and holiness of God as well as his New Testament love can thus be customarily declared in more contemporary speech, the case for retaining archaism in prayer will have lost its principal remaining prop.

The 'Gelineau' Psalms raise inescapably the issue of 'you' and 'thou' in direct address to God. To some, 'you' smacks of an unbecoming 'palliness with the Deity' (to use Dr H. H. Farmer's phrase). To others, 'thou' irretrievably consigns God to a realm outside our everyday world, whereas (they say) he has made it perfectly clear in Christ that he belongs within our everyday world. Some of the former are in all other respects in favour of modernizing the language, the thought-forms and the categories of prayer, but believe that 'thou' safeguards a necessary reverence which is dispelled by 'you'. The present compilers have come to the conviction that except in those parts of northern England where it remains a living mode of personal address, 'thou' contributes little except a sense of unreality and distance to any worshipper not already so accustomed to the usage that he mentally discounts it anyway. We believe that while it may indeed be necessary to teach people that 'distance' no less than 'proximity' is an ingredient of the Bible's picture of God, this is no way to do it. The use of archaic forms may seem a convenient means of inculcating the right attitude ready-made: but a habit formed by the by-passing of understanding is unlikely to have much value in the development of real spiritual maturity.

'But,' urge the objectors, 'once let in "you" and one has opened the door to all sorts of bathos and triviality.' This has sometimes been true in practice, but we cannot believe it is true of necessity. While we would not claim that modern English can preserve all the beauties and sonorities of 1611 or 1662, we are sure that it can express, with its own excellence, the truths and insights which alone make those beauties and sonorities religiously profitable. Besides, Christians of every language other than English worship in modern speech without loss either of reverence or of catholicity. Why should we think we cannot do the same?

To the question of catholicity we return below. First it is necessary to urge that 'thou' is in any case no guard against triviality, though it can sometimes disguise it and thus delay its exposure. What is true, however, is that there are some familiar constructions of liturgical language which are themselves unacceptable in modern English.[1] One such is the Collect form, in which the opening address to God is expanded by a relative clause indicating the special grounds on which we approach him. For example, 'O God, who hast prepared for them that love thee such good things as pass man's understanding . . .' In contemporary usage such (originally Latin) syntax cannot be employed without incongruity. We understand that a recent American collection, failing to reckon with this, has already been dubbed *The 'You Who' Missal*.

Does this mean, then, that the use of modern English in public worship must deprive the congregation of the devotional treasures of the past, and cut it off from catholic liturgical tradition? We do not think it does. Although a mixture of styles within a single prayer is not satisfactory,[2] we have found that a mixture of styles as between different sections of the same service is quite acceptable to congregations. They are, after all, already accustomed to the mixture of modern Bible readings and traditional hymn lyrics. Each *group* of prayers should be consistent in style. But we do not think that a desire, say, to retain the Collects in their Elizabethan form should dissuade anyone from using contemporary language for other prayers in the same service.

Prayers originally written in languages other than English can be perfectly well translated afresh (cf. Hamman's *Early Christian Prayers*, cited above). When this is attempted, however, we begin to encounter a much more serious set of problems. The true content of the material is sometimes found to be less apt to our use today than its beautiful Tudor apparel had led us to suppose. The 'Aaronic blessing', for

[1] Conversely (and this, we think, is even more important), there are many words and phrases which ought to be usable in public prayer today which are quite incompatible with 'thou' and its attendant verb-forms. See, for example, pp. 26-27.
[2] We have made an exception in the case of the responses at the Lord's Supper. There are formidable difficulties in the way of making congregationally usable any variation from the seventeenth-century form of the 'Sursum corda' and the 'Sanctus'. We have therefore incorporated their traditional English form in an otherwise modern English eucharistic prayer – though in another prayer we have attempted a new form for them.

instance, with its wonderfully attractive 'The Lord make his face to shine upon thee', is not nearly so suitable for Christian worship when put into language which shows how materialistic it really is. Yet the Authorized Version form remains a good blessing in its own right. Is one, then, to modernize the original, or the AV's sympathetic misrepresentation, or neither? We have attempted the first, and incorporated the result into our Orders for Baptism and Christian Marriage: but not without hesitation.

Nowhere does this problem become more acute than in the matter of the Lord's Prayer. Here, particularly in the final pair of petitions, it seems to us that it is impossible to translate the meaning of Matthew's or Luke's Greek simply by translating the words. Yet for congregational use a paraphrase of the prayer will hardly do: and even if it would, such questions would still remain as, for instance, which of the possible lines to take on what Jesus meant by 'the test', and whether contemporary Christians should be expected to pray to be saved from an 'Evil One' whose personal existence is not an article of faith. The *New English Bible* raises, but does not help to answer, such questions. We have thought it right to include, in the Appendix, not only a translation of the Lord's Prayer which could be used congregationally, but also some paraphrases which, we hope, begin to point towards the meaning of the petitions in modern English.

Questions of archaism and construction, then, important though they are, are not the only ones which must be raised today about the language of worship. It is more than a matter of finding new clothes for perennial thoughts. The categories we all use in framing our prayers, the mental diagrams we have about what is happening when we pray, and about what we expect to happen as a result, are themselves in question. If, for example, one wishes to express in modern terms the petition, 'We beseech thee to hear us, O Lord', one has not only to deal with the 'thee' and the 'O' and find a modern equivalent for 'beseech': one has also to consider whether the supplicant-to-potentate type of relationship presupposed by 'beseech' (in any language) has still any significance for western democratic man and, if so, whether that significance is any longer theologically defensible in the context of prayer. Even the asking God to 'hear' us is questionable, not so much because it is anthropomorphic (the language of prayer is bound to be that), but because it suggests the possibility, surely inadmissible, that God might not be as ready to hear as we to pray. It will be apparent that in this book we have scarcely done more than scratch the surface of this problem of thought-forms and what we have called mental diagrams: but it has been constantly in mind, and we think it is by far the most important of the issues confronting liturgists today.

We have not felt tied, in the course of the book, to any one modern translation of the Bible, though we have usually gone first to the *New English Bible* and the *Revised Standard Version*. One prayer (p. 20) is firmly wedded to the 'Gelineau' version of a Psalm: but in most instances it will be found a simple matter to modify the wording, if necessary, to match the translation being used for the readings.

Some of us would have liked to include a greater number and variety of responsive prayers; but to go beyond the simple type in which a single memorable response is used throughout a prayer involves putting a book in the hands of the congregation, and it was not in that rôle that we thought our work could be of the most use at this moment. We urge that when a versicle and response are to be used they should be clearly announced, preferably twice over, immediately before the prayer in which they occur.

Each of us has contributed prayers which he has used in public worship. After general discussion these have been revised, in the light of criticism, by their writers in company with at least one other of the compilers. This procedure has been followed in every case except that of the complete Orders of Service in Part II, which were prepared by all of us together. Finally the manuscript was submitted to an assessor, who had had no part in its production, and who could thus form an independent judgment about the acceptability of particular words and phrases over which the compilers might have been too lenient to each other. We are grateful to Dr Erik Routley of Edinburgh for doing this for us, and we have adopted many of his suggestions: but the responsibility for the book's contents rests not upon him but upon the compilers collectively.

Acknowledgments

The compilers and publishers wish to acknowledge their indebtedness to the following, who have kindly given permission for the use of copyright material:

The Oxford and Cambridge University Presses, for verses and phrases from *The New English Bible, New Testament*; Messrs Thomas Nelson & Sons, Ltd., for verses and phrases from the *Revised Standard Version of the Bible*, copyrighted 1946 and 1952; Canon J. B. Phillips and Messrs Geoffrey Bles, Ltd., for verses and phrases from *The New Testament in Modern English*; and The Grail (England), for verses and phrases from *The Psalms: A New Translation*.

PART I

Material for General Use

Opening Prayers

1 P18

Lord God, we come to adore you. You are the ground of all that is.
You hold us in being, and without you we could not be.
Before we were born, before time began, before the universe came
 into being, you were.
When time is finished, when the universe is no more, you will still be.
Nothing can take your power from you.
And in your presence we can only be silent before the mystery of
 your being, for no words of ours can do justice to your grandeur.

(A silence)

Yet you have spoken to us. Out of universal silence your living word
 has sprung.
You have spoken, and given form and beauty to the world.
You have spoken, and given purpose to human life.
You have spoken, and declared the forgiveness of our sin.
You have spoken, and freed us from the fear of death.

Lord Jesus Christ, divine Word, speak to us now.
Show us the beauty of life; unite us to the eternal purpose; remove
 our guilt; conquer the fear of death in our hearts.
Speak and let us hear, for your name's sake.

2

People ought to praise you, God of earth and heaven.
All of us ought to praise you.
 You are always there, never growing old, fresh as each new day:
 You were in Jesus, showing us your love by his death, and by his
 resurrection giving us hope of living with you for ever:

CPPW B

You bring life and light to the world by your Holy Spirit, making
every moment your moment, and every day your day of coming
to the rescue.
To God the Father, God the Son, God the Holy Spirit let all the
world give praise, today, and every day, and for ever and ever.

3

Father, we come to you now
in silence, yet shouting for joy.

We come in silence
overawed by the thought of your love for us.
You rule supreme over time and space,
yet you loved us so much that you gave your only Son
to suffer and die for us.
To think that you love us like that
takes our breath away.
We are struck dumb.
There is nothing we can say.

(A silence)

And yet, we cannot stay silent
when we think of your love for us.
You gave us new birth into a living hope
when you brought Jesus back from death;
so that we could make a new start in life
free from the guilt and shame of the past,
confident that nothing in death or life
can separate us from your love.
To think that you love us like that
makes us long to break our silence
– to shout for joy and to sing your praise.

Father, accept our worship and praise
both silent and spoken
through Jesus Christ our Lord.

4

Let us remember God, everlastingly great, utterly loving, wholly to
be trusted.
And because God knows us through and through,
  because God loves us better than we love ourselves,
  because we need not and cannot pretend to him,
    let us quietly acknowledge our need of his forgiveness and
    renewal.

(A silence)

God, have mercy on me, sinner that I am.

(A silence)

Jesus said: 'This man, I tell you, went home acquitted of his sins.'
And Paul wrote: 'If God is on our side, who is against us?
  He did not spare his own Son but surrendered him for us all.
  With this gift how can he fail to lavish on us all he has to give?
  Christ who died and was raised from the dead is at God's right hand
    and pleads our cause.
We are at peace with God through our Lord Jesus Christ.'

5

Holy Spirit, hear us as we pray.
  Take the faltering and stumbling words we say
    and turn them into songs.
  So you will help us give to God
    the praise we want to give.

Holy Spirit, speak to us as we pray.
  Bring merciful and forgiving words today
    from God the Father.
  So you will help us find in him
    the peace we need to find.

Holy Spirit, come to us today.
  Tell of the dying and rising of Christ the Lord
    and give us joy.
  So you will help us live for God
    the life we ought to live.

Through Jesus Christ our Lord.

6

*This prayer is based on the 'Gelineau' translation of Psalm 95 (96).
To the words,* 'Give the Lord glory and power', *the response is,*
  'Give the Lord the glory of his name'.

P 4 0 . O sing a new song to the Lord: sing to the Lord all the earth.
  O sing to the Lord, bless his name: proclaim his help day by day.
  Give the Lord, you families of peoples,
    Give the Lord glory and power:
    People: Give the Lord the glory of his name.

It is the Lord who has brought us together to pray, and praise him,
and receive his instruction.
    Give the Lord glory and power:
    People: Give the Lord the glory of his name.

It is the Lord who has shown his great love for us,
and has taught us, through Christ, to call him 'Father'.
    Give the Lord glory and power:
    People: Give the Lord the glory of his name.

It is the Lord who gives us strength to do our work and earn our
living, and leisure to enjoy the results of our work.
    Give the Lord glory and power:
    People: Give the Lord the glory of his name.

It is the Lord who enables us to harness the world's resources
to provide warmth, and power, and machines to reduce life's drudgery.
 Give the Lord glory and power:
 People: Give the Lord the glory of his name.

It is the Lord who enlarges our vision by the work of artists and
craftsmen, and the deeds of courageous men and women.
 Give the Lord glory and power:
 People: Give the Lord the glory of his name.

Bring an offering and enter his courts: worship the Lord in his
temple.
O earth, tremble before him: proclaim to the nations, 'God is King'.

7

Lord, we believe you are always ready to hear our prayers.
We do not ask you to give us anything which you know will not be
 for our good.
Therefore help us, please, to understand what you want, and to ask
 for that.

8

We praise you, Creator, our Father: we acknowledge your control of
 the world.
We confess ourselves believers who have sinned: we come to you
 forgiving one another.
Reassure us of forgiveness; reassure us of your help; re-engage us
 in your service: because of Jesus Christ our Lord.

9

Lord, you are our God.
We want to realize how much we depend upon you.
You have not only given us life,
    you have made us able to think about its meaning
    and to choose and work for what is good.
In the world much is confusing;
    many voices strive to be heard.
Yet we have your word to guide us,
    the life and teaching of your Son,
    the example of many faithful Christians.
We have known your hand holding us fast,
    your steps marking out the way for us:
    we long to know you still.
Your presence transforms even the darker times:
    with you we need not be afraid.
Nothing can separate us from your love.
Draw out from us such an answering love
    that in our time of testing we may not fall away.

✗ **10** *16/6/68.*

Lord God, your eyes are open day and night watching your children;
your ears are always ready to listen to their prayer. We have come to
worship you. We come as sinners, in need of your forgiveness. We
come tired from our work, in need of refreshment and recreation.
We come with worries, in need of your guidance. But first, please
lift us out of our preoccupation with our own needs. Allow us to see
you with the eyes of faith, and to hear with understanding what you
say to us. Make us thankful for all the good we have received from
you. Awaken in us a longing to do what is right. And make us aware
of the great company, past, present and to come, with whom we join
to worship you.

11

As on a first day you began the work of creating us;
As on a first day you raised your Son from the dead;
So on this first day, good Lord, freshen and remake us:
And as the week is new, let our lives begin again
Because of Jesus who shows us your loving power.

12

Our God, how great you are! On the first day of the week we commemorate your creation of the world and all that is in it.
Thank you for the light which wakes us morning by morning,
and for that greater light which shines in Jesus Christ.

Our God, how great you are! On the first day of the week you raised Jesus from the dead.
Raise us with him to a new quality of faith and life.

Our God, how great you are! Again on the first day of the week you sent your Spirit on your disciples.
Do not deprive us of your Spirit,
but renew him in us day by day.

13

Lord our God, great, eternal, wonderful, utterly to be trusted: you give life to us all, you help those who come to you, you give hope to those who appeal to you. Forgive our sins, secret and open, and rid us of every habit of thought which is foreign to the gospel. Set our hearts and consciences at peace, so that we may bring our prayers to you confidently and without fear; through Jesus Christ our Lord.

(Based on a prayer from the Coptic Liturgy of St Basil)

14

P41 Lord God, you are a refuge and a strength for us, a helper close at hand in time of distress. So we shall not be afraid.

If the foundations of our lives are shaken: we shall not be afraid.
If the familiar landmarks of life disappear: we shall not be afraid.
If confusion threatens and annihilation is near: we shall not be afraid.

For you, Lord of hosts, are with us:
You, God of Jacob, are our refuge.

Lord, we remember what you have done.

When we were lost in the world's confusion: Jesus Christ found us.
When we were overcome by the pointlessness of it all: Jesus Christ gave purpose to our life.
When death and destruction had done their worst: Jesus Christ was raised from death, and showed us that you are still in control.

You are God, supreme in the universe, unshakable foundation of our being.
You have raised our Lord and Saviour Jesus Christ from death.
And so, whatever happens, we shall not be afraid.

For you, Lord of hosts, are with us:
You, God of Jacob, are our refuge.

(Based on Psalm 46)

15

How great is your name, Lord our God, through all the earth!
Your majesty is praised above the heavens.

When we see the vastnesses of space, all of your making,
the galaxies and stars you have arranged,
we are amazed that you keep us in mind,
that you care for us mortal men.

Yet, you have made us in your image;
   you have caused Jesus Christ to appear among us,
   and we are crowned with glory and honour because of his
      suffering and death.
   You have put all things under his feet.

We thank you, God, for bringing mankind to its destined greatness
   through Jesus Christ.
How great is your name, Lord our God, through all the earth!
Glory to you, for ever!

(Based on Psalm 8)

16

(Especially when children are present)

Most wonderful and loving God   YP 2.
we praise you
we worship you
we thank you
   for everything you have given us.

We thank you for life itself
and for everything that makes life worth living:
   for the things we like to eat,
   for the things we like to do,
   for the people who love us and care for us.

But as we say thank-you now
we know that we do not always say thank-you
in the way we live our lives.

We are sorry as we remember
   the wrong things we have done,
   the things we should not have said,
   and the ways we have hurt other people.

Most wonderful and loving God
   forgive us for everything that is wrong in our lives.
By the power of the Holy Spirit
   help us to live as Jesus lived,
   so that we may say thank-you for your gifts
   in everything we say and do.

We ask it in his name.

17

(*Especially when children are present*)

Here we are, our Father.
You called us, and we've come.
You want us to learn some more about your love for us,
   and we want your help to make our lives less selfish and more
     loving.
So we have come to church
   to listen to what you have to say to us,
   to give you thanks for what you do for us,
   and to share with you the hopes you have given us through Jesus.
Help us to make good use of our time together:
   and when we leave here again help us to take our worship home
     with us.
Through Jesus Christ our Lord.

18

(*Especially when children are present*)

Father God, we sing our praise and thanks to you: for you are our
   friend.
You love us and look after us, and nothing happens without your
   noticing.
You keep on being kind to us, however little we deserve it.

In Jesus you show us the right way to behave:
and if we trust you, you help us to live as your family.
So everyone who knows you thanks you and loves you. Together we
thank you now.
Father, help your children everywhere to grow up and to grow
together.
As we follow the example of Jesus may we get wiser:
and not only wiser, but also more loving.
Through our life in your family may we learn unselfishness,
and be ready to make sacrifices for your sake.

19

At the Lord's Supper

Lord God, we are glad to come here today.
Gladly we come to give you thanks
for everything you have done for us.
Gladly we come to sing and pray
and listen to what you say to us.
But we are most glad and thankful
because you have invited us to come to the table of our Lord
Jesus Christ
and eat bread with him.

We know as we come to worship you
that we have failed to be what we ought to be,
that we do not live as we ought to live.
We do not deserve to be here at all.

Lord God, forgive us.
Pour out your Holy Spirit into our lives
to give us peace
and the strength to leave self behind
take up the cross
and follow Christ
today, tomorrow and always.
In his name we ask it.

20

At the Lord's Supper

l c Ham .
re|2|73.
11.23 pm .

Jesus said: 'I did not come to invite virtuous people, but sinners.'
(Mark 2.17 NEB)

Merciful God, we do not dare to come to this table
   trusting in our own goodness and virtue.

We come because we are sinful men and need forgiveness.
We come because we are hungry for life and need to be fed.
   Father, forgive us and feed us.

We come because Christ has invited us sinners.
We come in gratitude and wonder
   to offer our very selves to you
   in worship and adoration.
      Father, accept our praise.

Through Jesus Christ our Lord.

Thanksgiving

Our help is in the name of the Lord, who made heaven & earth
Jesus said "Where two or three are gathered together in my name, there am
Let us pray. I in the midst of them"

I

P9.

We thank you, God, that you have always loved the world you have
  made.

We thank you that in Jesus this love of yours was fully expressed. P18

We thank you that he was known as the friend of those whom most
  men despised, and that he shared his plans and his work with
  ordinary men and women like ourselves.

We thank you for the honour of being called his friends, and we
  pray that we may *never* let him down.

We know that this friendship *does* not always seemed real to us.

We are sorry that we ~~are so often worried~~ *worry so much that we are so selfish, that we forget you so often* as if your love were *not* there. *at all*

We are sorry, too, that we do so little to make your friendship real
  to other people.

We pray that we may be forgiven, and that you will show us how we
  may be better friends and followers of Jesus.

For his name's sake.

And grant each Jesus a sense of your presence, now, that what we do
together in this place may be done as in your sight. We believe that you
are the God of new beginnings, & this is a new beginning tonight
for these young people. Without your help & blessing we cannot do anything

Let us thank God for his courage in making mankind at all. *right. So bless us*

Let us thank him for giving us knowledge of good and evil, *now, that all may*
  and for allowing us freedom of choice. *be done to the praise of*
  your glory "

Let us thank him for not overruling our freedom for our own good.

Father, it seems to us courageous of you to make a creature who
  might refuse your love.

When he did so, you never changed your mind about him,
  but stood by your first intention.

We praise you for thinking man worth redeeming,
and for wanting him not as a slave but as a friend.
Through Jesus your Son, you have enabled us to trust your love:
show us your will as well; and give us the courage to act on it –
always.

3

Heavenly Father, you are altogether good.
You never do less than justice to men:
instead, you always do us more than justice –
showing kindness when we have no right to expect it,
and repeatedly overlooking what we owe you.

Often we find you forgiving people who to us seem even greater
sinners than ourselves.
Help us not to be grudging and resentful about this.
Deliver us from being so blind to the purpose of your generosity
that we call it unfairness.
Rather, may we imitate your love by loving one another, so that
we can safely pray as we have been commanded, 'Forgive us our
debts, as we forgive our debtors'.

And let the light of your glory in the face of Jesus dawn upon us
every day, so that we can see how wide the horizons of life and
hope and service really are.
Let all time and all eternity give glory to you
through Jesus Christ our Lord.

4

Lord Jesus Christ, our great High Priest, merciful and faithful,
we are glad that you were made like us,
that you passed through the test of suffering,
that you were made perfect through suffering.

Humbly and joyfully we thank you for offering yourself to God as
   the perfect sacrifice,
   to cleanse our consciences and make us fit to serve God.
We thank you that by dying you broke the power of death,
   and that you live to intercede on our behalf.
Grant our request that today and throughout our lives
   we may approach God through you with confidence,
   and hold fast to the faith we profess.

5

We thank you, Lord our God, for creating the world
   and for preserving it until now.
We thank you for the regular return of day and night, and of the
   seasons,
   and for the dependability of nature and of time.
We thank you for memory, which enables us to build on the experience of the past;
   for imagination, which admits us to a wider world than we could
      otherwise know;
   and for foresight, by which we plan for the future.
We thank you for your patience with the errors and sins of mankind:
   you have neither wearied of us nor allowed us to ruin ourselves
      in self-destruction or utter degradation,
   but have sent your Son Jesus Christ to break down the barriers
      between us and you and between us and each other,
      and to restore the broken unity of human life.

6

We thank you, God, for all the variety of the human race.
We thank you for our dependence on other people's skill, labour and
   love.
We are glad that our experience is enriched by men and women from
   every walk of life, of every colour, language and belief.
We praise you for the development and unfolding of human character.

Most of all we thank you that Jesus lived a human life, as our example, our teacher and our saviour.
May we learn the most valuable lessons from life, and become useful servants of our fellow men.

7

In this prayer, after the words, 'Father, we lift up our hearts', *all say together*, 'And bring you our worship and praise'.

PW.

Lord God our Father,
most wonderful, most gracious, most glorious God,
we praise and adore you for all that you have done for us in Jesus Christ.

Because though the divine nature was his from the first,
yet he did not think to snatch at equality with you,
but made himself nothing, assuming the nature of a slave:
Father, we lift up our hearts,
All: And bring you our worship and praise.

Because bearing the human likeness, revealed in human shape,
he humbled himself, and in obedience accepted even death,
death on a cross:
Father, we lift up our hearts,
All: And bring you our worship and praise.

Because you raised him to the heights, and bestowed on him the name above all names, that at the name of Jesus every knee should bow, in heaven, on earth, and in the depths, and every tongue confess that he is Lord:
Father, we lift up our hearts,
All: And bring you our worship and praise.

Worthy is the Lamb that was slain to receive all power and wealth,
   wisdom and might, honour and glory and praise!
Praise and honour, glory and might, to him who sits on the throne,
   and to the Lamb, for ever and ever.

(Based on Phil. 2.5-11 NEB, *and Rev. 5.12, 13* NEB)

8

In this prayer, after the words, 'With all our heart and mind', *all say together,* 'We thank you, Lord'.

Mighty God,
we lift up our hearts and praise you
for the unlimited power of your love in Jesus Christ.

Because he never stopped loving you
   even when his disciples ran away
   and death stared him in the face:
because he never stopped loving other people
   even when he was being nailed to the cross:
      With all our heart and mind
      All: We thank you, Lord.

Because the worst that men could do
   in sending Jesus out to die
   could not stand in the way of your love:
because you showed us the power of your love
   in raising him from death:
      With all our heart and mind
      All: We thank you, Lord.

Because by his dying and rising again
   we know that your love is strong enough
   to go on loving till the end of time:

because we know for certain
 that your love must win in the end:
  With all our heart and mind
  All: We thank you, Lord.

P1. Mighty God,
 we lift up our hearts to you
 in gratitude for your love to us.
Take our lives –
 our work and our leisure,
 the ordinary things of life and the special things,
 the sadness and joy we know and have known.
Accept, we pray, our praise and thanksgiving
 as we offer our very selves to you
 in worship and adoration.

Through Jesus Christ our Lord.

Confession

1   16/6/68.

✝ We confess to you, Lord, what we are:
    we are not the people we like others to think we are;
    we are afraid to admit even to ourselves what lies in the depths of
      our souls.
But we do not want to hide our true selves from you.
We believe that you know us as we are, and yet you love us.
Help us not to shrink from self-knowledge;
    teach us to respect ourselves for your sake;
    give us the courage to put our trust in your guiding and power.

We also confess to you, Lord, the unrest of the world,
    to which we contribute and in which we share.
Forgive us that so many of us are indifferent to the needs of our
    fellow men.
Forgive our reliance on weapons of terror,
    our discrimination against people of different race,
    and our preoccupation with material standards.
And forgive us Christians for being so unsure of our good news
    and so unready to tell it. ✝

Raise us out of the paralysis of guilt into the freedom and energy of
    forgiven people.
And for those who through long habit find forgiveness hard to accept,
    we ask you to break their bondage and set them free.
Through Jesus Christ our Lord.

2

We confess to you, Lord, that we have not only disobeyed your law,
  but have neglected and spurned your gospel.
Our sins are forgiven; we are your children; no one can snatch us
  out of your hand; in Christ we are more than conquerors over sin
  and circumstance.
But we have only half-believed these things.
Forgive us that our lives are so poor, when they should always be
  proclaiming your praises.
Make us so glad about all you have done that we cannot keep silent.
Form our characters so that they bring you credit.
Through Jesus Christ our Lord.

3

God our Father,
  we have sinned against you
  in thought, word and deed:
  we have not loved you with all our heart;
  we have not loved our neighbour as ourselves.
But you have kept faith with us.
Have mercy on us;
  strip us of all that is un-Christian;
  and help us to live up to our calling;
  through Jesus Christ our Lord.

4

Lord, please forgive our sins,
  and set us free from them.

We confess to the sin of *pride*:
  we have been sure of our own goodness and importance
  and have looked down on others.
Help us to appreciate the true worth of other people.

We confess to the sin of *envy*:
   we have been displeased when others have been more
      successful or sought after than we have been.
Help us to be glad when others prosper.

We confess to the sin of *anger*:
   we have lost our temper
   and nursed grievances.
Help us to be patient and understanding with everyone.

We confess to the sin of *self-indulgence*:
   we have had enough and to spare,
   yet have neglected the needs of others.
Help us to deny ourselves
   so that others may not be in want.

We confess to the sin of *unchastity*:
   in one way or another we have used sex wrongly.
Help us to create and uphold right relations between men and
      women,
   inside marriage and outside it.

We confess to the sin of *anxiety*:
   we have worried about many things.
Help us to trust you to see us through.

We confess to the sin of *laziness*:
   we have been lukewarm Christians.
Make us eager to do your will.

5

Pq. Merciful God,
we confess to you now
that we have sinned.

We confess
the sins that no one knows
and the sins that everyone knows:
the sins that are a burden to us
and the sins that do not bother us
because we have got used to them.

We confess our sins as a church.
We have not loved one another
as Christ loved us.
We have not forgiven one another
as we have been forgiven.
We have not given ourselves
in love and service for the world
as Christ gave himself for us.

Father, forgive us.
Send the Holy Spirit to us,
that he may give us power to live
as, by your mercy,
you have called us to live.

Through Jesus Christ our Lord.

6

In this prayer, after the words, 'In the name of Jesus Christ', *all say together,* 'Father, forgive us and help us'.　P18.

Father,
we ask forgiveness for everything that is wrong in our lives.

If we have a grievance against anyone,
if we are jealous of somebody,
if we are resentful and bitter about anything:
　　In the name of Jesus Christ,
　　All: Father, forgive us and help us.

If we have hurt or offended others
　or treated other people unfairly:
　　In the name of Jesus Christ,
　　All: Father, forgive us and help us.

If we have gone back on our word
　or forgotten to keep our promises;
if we have been dishonest or deceitful:
　　In the name of Jesus Christ,
　　All: Father, forgive us and help us.

Help us to see and admit all our faults
　and make amends where we can.

May we be so secure in the knowledge of your forgiveness and love
that we become free to forget our pride,
　let go of resentment,
and be at peace with you,
with other people, and with ourselves.

Through Jesus Christ our Lord.

7

God, our Father, we admit to you that we have failed to be the men and women you meant us to be.

When duty has called we have shirked it, and we have defended ourselves with excuses which did not convince us, let alone deceive you.

We are sorry for our failure, which has hurt ourselves as well as others, and we resolve to put right what can be put right.

And as for those mistakes which cannot be changed and constantly accuse us, we surrender them to you. Save us from being haunted by them. Release us from their burden, so that we can step into the future unafraid, knowing that, even if we fail, failure does not put us out of reach of your help, which comes to us through Jesus Christ our Lord.

8

God, our Father, we find it difficult to come to you, because our knowledge of you is so imperfect.

In our ignorance we have imagined you to be our enemy; we have wrongly thought that you take pleasure in punishing our sins; and we have foolishly conceived you to be a tyrant over human life.

And we confess that, when life has ill-treated us, we have felt grievance and resentment against you.

But since Jesus came among us, we have realized that all this is fantasy, which we have imagined because we did not know you.

He has shown us that you are loving, that you are on our side against all that stunts life, and that our resentment against you was groundless.

So we come to you, asking you to forgive our past ignorance, and wanting to know more and more of you through Jesus Christ our Lord.

9

We confess, Lord, that we have not loved you or our neighbour as we should. We have often neglected opportunities of good: sometimes we have done actual harm. Our consciences accuse us over trifles, but let us stay blind to your weightier demands. We know that a mere apology will not do. We resolve to turn from the sins we know. We ask you to show us the sins we do not recognize. We resolve to forgive any who have wronged us; and to seek reconciliation with any from whom we are estranged. And now we beg your pardon and ask your help.

10

Heavenly Father, we admit the mistakes of our life which we cannot undo. Help us to accept their consequences without bitterness, and within their limits to see our immediate obedience, and to act upon it with joy. Through Jesus Christ, our Lord.

Assurance of Forgiveness

1

'Here are words you may trust,
words that merit full acceptance:
"Christ Jesus came into the world to save sinners".'

To all who confess their sins
and resolve to lead a new life
he says:
   'Your sins are forgiven',

and he also says:
   'Follow me'.

'Now to the King of all worlds,
immortal, invisible, the only wise God,
be honour and glory for ever and ever. Amen.'

(The first and last quotations are from I Tim. 1.15, 17 NEB)

2

Listen –
here is good news:
'Christ Jesus came into the world to save sinners'[1]
– to forgive you in your failure
– to accept you as you are
– to set you free from evil's power
   and make you what you were meant to be.

[1] *I Tim. 1.15* NEB.

Listen to him,
for through him his Father says
to all who come to him, as you have come to him:
   'You are accepted.
   You are forgiven.
   I will set you free.'

'O depth of wealth, wisdom, and knowledge in God!
How unsearchable his judgments, how untraceable his ways!...
Source, Guide, and Goal of all that is –
to him be glory for ever!
Amen.'[1]

[1] *Romans 11.33, 36* NEB.

Supplication and Intercession

✗ 1 16/6/68.

Lord Christ, crucified for us,
  help us to love, as you have loved
  help us to live, as you have lived
  help us to be neighbours to our fellow man in his need
    as you in your mercy were neighbour to us
    and suffered and died for us.
In your name we ask it. ✗

(*Based on Luke 10.36f.* NEB)

2

Father,
as we go to our homes and our work this coming week
we ask you to send the Holy Spirit into our lives.

Open our ears	– to hear what you are saying to us in the things that happen to us and in the people we meet.
Open our eyes	– to see the needs of the people round us.
Open our hands	– to do our work well to help when help is needed.
Open our lips	– to tell others the good news of Jesus and bring comfort, happiness and laughter to other people.
Open our minds	– to discover new truth about you and the world.

Open our hearts   – to love you and our fellow men
                      as you have loved us in Jesus.

To him, with you our Father and the Holy Spirit, one God,
all honour and praise shall be given
now and for ever.

Ϟ ₓ 3 16/6/68.
Lord Jesus Christ,
    you are the light of the world:
    light up our lives when we are in darkness.

In the darkness of our uncertainty –
    when we don't know what to do,
    when decisions are hard to take:
Lord, give us light to guide us.

In the darkness of our anxiety –
    when we are worried about what the future may bring,
    when we don't know where to turn:
Lord, give us the light of your peace.

In the darkness of our despair –
    when life seems empty,
    when we feel there is no point in going on:
Lord, give us the light of your hope.

In your name we ask it.   ✘

In this prayer, after the words, 'Father, hear our prayer', *all say together,* 'That we may live in him'.

Listen to what the apostle Paul said:
'As therefore you received Christ Jesus the Lord,
so live in him, rooted and built up on him,
and established in the faith . . .
Put on the garments that suit God's chosen people.'

P9. Lord God our Father,
grant that as we have received Jesus Christ the Lord
so we may live in him.

That we may look upon the needs of others
and put on the compassion of Jesus Christ:
Father, hear our prayer
All: That we may live in him.

That we may put to death all arrogance and pride
and put on the humility of Jesus Christ:
Father, hear our prayer
All: That we may live in him.

That we may be set free from anger
and put on the patience of Jesus Christ:
Father, hear our prayer
All: That we may live in him.

That we may leave behind all bitterness and resentment
and put on the forgiveness of Jesus Christ:
Father, hear our prayer
All: That we may live in him.

46   *Supplication and Intercession*

And that in everything we do
    we may be filled with the love of Jesus Christ:
        Father, hear our prayer
        All: That we may live in him.

To him, with you our Father, and the Holy Spirit
we give all honour and praise
now and for ever.

(*Based on Colossians 2.6* RSV *and 3.12-13* NEB)

5

Lord God,
we praise you,
we worship you,
because by our baptism into the body of Christ
you have given us a new beginning,
    a new kind of life.

We know that much of our life
    – our thoughts, feelings, and actions –
has not yet been touched or changed
by the new life you have given:

help us to see the claims of your love
in every part of our life
and having seen them to accept them,
so that everything in us may be remade by your love.

Through Jesus Christ our Lord.

6

For God's kingdom

Eternal Father, you sent us your Son so that as he obeyed you perfectly your kingdom on earth could begin. Now that you have sent us the Spirit, help us to obey you as Christ did, so that your kingdom begun in him may be spread in us.

7

For peace

Show us, good Lord,
  the peace we should seek,
  the peace we must give,
  the peace we can keep,
  the peace we must forgo,
  and the peace you have given in Jesus our Lord.

8

For the Holy Spirit

Lord Jesus Christ, when you went to the Father you promised your men they would not be deserted but have the Holy Spirit in your place. Help us admit that we need him; give us the sense to recognize him; and make us more ready to rely on him; so that we live our lives in his continual company.

9

Lord Jesus, when you have drawn all men to yourself, there will be peace on earth.

When we try to get things for ourselves, and have things our own way, we fight and push, and are angry and cruel, and everything is made less happy than it was meant to be, and your kingdom does not come.

So give us your Spirit, to make us people who build your kingdom, not people who pull it down.

Help us to want things your way, not our way.

Take our strength and our energy, and help us to put all we have into the struggle for your goodness and your truth.

Yours be the power and the victory for ever and ever.

10

God, our life-giver and liberator, make us both alert and free in your service.

In the light of your truth may we see what value to set on each day's events, and how best to deploy our resources for each day's decisions.

Help us to be hard-headed without becoming hard-hearted: and if we have to choose between two evils, give us at least the will to do right, and the assurance that even when we are at our wits' end we are never out of your mercy's reach.

Through Jesus Christ our Lord.

11

Based on I Timothy 4.10 NEB: *'We have set our hope on the living God, who is the Saviour of all men – the Saviour, above all, of believers.'*

We have set our hope on you, our living God, as those who set course for home from distant places. But we need your help if we are to keep on course: we need fresh sight of you, on which to check our bearings. Let this service be a check-point for us. Show us where we are and where we should be. You are near as well as far – accompanying as well as beckoning: make this a meeting-place between our minds and your mind, so that we may see that the controlling interest in human affairs is yours.

CPPW D

P₁₁. Living God, you declare yourself to be the Saviour of all men. You know in full what we know only in part, how much men need a Saviour. If you do not rescue us from our egotism and complacency, who will? If you do not purify our motives, and shake us out of the sentimentality of our usual hopes and fears, who will? May your declared purpose get through to the world today, our Father.

Living God, you declare yourself to be the Saviour, above all, of believers. In every country in the world are men and women who believe that your word in Jesus Christ holds promise not only for this life but for the life to come. Save your believers from spiritual arrogance: save them equally from dismay at the force of all that they are up against. Show them how to have divided opinions without having divided loyalties. May your declared purpose get through to the Church today, our Father.

There are too many whose lives are crippled and inhibited by illness, ignorance, bitterness and grief; by exploitation and by envy, by physical or mental handicap. We know and love some of these: you know and love them all. Take them into the care and skill of your own hands: help us all to be your own hands: so that everything that happens may come to serve the purposes of your love, and your design for humanity may be fulfilled in all its beauty, through Jesus Christ our Lord.

12

For others (*Suitable for use after a series of specific biddings*)

Hear our prayer, Father,
   for all in whom trust has been placed,
    all to whom power is given,
    all from whom love is asked,
    all through whom wisdom is sought,
   and all by whom joy can come
    because of Jesus our Lord.

13

For those who neglect God

We pray for any who neglect you, Father:
    for any who have gone the wrong way,
    especially those who have brought trouble on themselves and
      others.
Take from them all blindness and stubbornness.
Give them hope and strength to begin again.
And make other people loving and wise enough to help them.

14

For the Church

Eternal God, you know the failure of the Church better than we do,
    for you have founded it to be yours.
Stop us from treating it as ours.
Re-establish your right over it and make it serve you.
May your will be most done where your name is most hallowed.

15

For family life

Father in heaven, give to all parents the resources they require.
Help them to fulfil their promises and keep their hopes.
Strengthen them in difficulty and disappointment.
And make the home of every child a model of your kingdom,
    the care of every parent a parable of your love.

Jesus, Son of God, you loved us and sacrificed yourself for us. God forbid that we should boast in anything except your Cross. May we be crucified with you, be set free from the narrow and selfish standards of the world, and experience the liberty of children of God. May we cease to live for ourselves, and live for you who for our sake died and rose again.

Jesus, Shepherd and Guardian of our souls, by your sufferings you set us an example: it is for us to follow in your steps. May we follow you in your patience and your forgiveness, not shrink from sharing your baptism and your cup, and give ourselves in sacrificial service to mankind.

Jesus, Head of the Church, you gave yourself up for the Church, so that it might be holy and without blemish. Cleanse and renew by your word the whole body of the Church, so that it may enjoy the peace and unity you want it to have, and not be slack in carrying out its mission to mankind.

Jesus, Good Shepherd, you laid down your life to gather the scattered children of God and to draw all men to yourself. Bring home to the hearts and consciences of men the reality of your love and the meaning of your sacrifice, so that they may gladly give themselves to you and receive the benefits of your passion.

Jesus, by your death you broke down the barriers between Jew and Gentile, Greek and barbarian, male and female, slave and freeman. Heal the tragic divisions of our world, between East and West, black and white, Arab and Jew, so that each man may respect his brother as someone for whom you died.

Jesus, by God's gracious will you have gone through death for every man and destroyed its power. May all who profess themselves Christians have such faith in you, that they may not fear the hour of their death, but with reverent hope look upon it as the entrance to fuller life.

P13.
Jesus, you proved your Father's love to us by dying for us while we were still sinners. Arouse in us an answering love, ready to work, to speak, to think or to suffer in obedience to your perfect will.

17

We pray, Lord God, for your Church throughout the world: **P9,**
that it may share to the full in the work of your Son,
revealing you to men
and reconciling men to you;
that Christians may learn to love one another,
as you have loved us;
that your Church may more and more exhibit the unity
which is your will and your gift.

We pray that we and all Christians
may be what you want us to be,
and do what you want us to do:
that we may be content with whatever comes our way,
and attain peace of mind in self-forgetfulness.

We pray for those who suffer for faith and conviction,
and are tempted to turn back
because their way is hard:
help and strengthen them, Lord,
so that they may hold out to the end,
and by their loyal witness draw others to you.

We pray for our country:
that none may exploit others,
and none be neglected or forgotten;
that we may be quick to reward service
and to recognize true worth;
and that all may work for the common life and welfare.

We pray for the life of the world:
  that every nation may seek the way that leads to peace;
  that human rights and freedom may everywhere be respected;
  and that the world's resources may be ungrudgingly shared.

We pray for the homes of mankind:
  that husbands and wives may accept lifelong marriage as their
    ideal.
We pray for broken homes
    and those in danger of breaking,
  that your love may redeem and remake them.
We pray for the homeless,
  that no family may have to face a lifetime without a home.

We pray for those who are ill:
  that illness may not break their spirit;
  that through the healing skill you have given
    they may be made well;
  and that those who are permanently handicapped
    may find the way to use and overcome their suffering.

Finally, we pray that the Gospel of our Lord Jesus Christ may be
  known and accepted by increasing numbers of men.
Draw to yourself all seekers after truth and goodness:
  may they find the unfathomable riches
    which can be found in you alone.
And may all the nations you have made
  come and worship you
  and honour your name.

✗ Father, you do not create us to live alone
    and you have not made us all alike.
We thank you for the varied society of mankind,
    into which we come,
    by which we are brought up,
    and through which we discover your purpose for our lives.
In gratitude we pray for our fellow men.

We pray for our families,
    with whom we live day by day.
May this most searching test of our character
    not find us broken and empty.
By all that we do and say
    help us to build up the faith and confidence
      of those we love.
When we quarrel, help us to forgive quickly.
Help us to welcome new members into our families without reserve,
    and not to neglect those who in our eyes have become less interest-
      ing or more demanding.

We pray for the places where we work,
    that there we may be workmen who have no need to be ashamed.
We ask to be reliable rather than successful,
    worthy of trust rather than popular.
Whether those we work with be many or few,
    may we help to give them the sense that they are personally
      wanted and cared for.

We pray for the communities to which we belong,
    that we may be good citizens.
Make us willing to accept responsibility
      when we are called to it;
    make us willing also to give place to others,
      that they too may have their opportunity.
Grant that our influence may be good and not evil.

We pray for the generation to which we belong,
  those with whom we share a common fund of memory,
    common standards of behaviour
    and a common attitude towards the world.
Grant that the presence of Christ may be so real to us that we may
  be able to help our generation to see him also as our contemporary.

Father, into whose world we come
  and from whose world finally we must go:
  we thank you for all those people,
    great and humble,
    who have maintained the fabric of the world's life in the past
    and left us a great inheritance.
May we take up and encourage what is good,
  and hand it on to those who come after,
  believing that our work in your name will not be wasted. ✗

19

Lord God, the story of your love for us makes us realize that there
are many others as well as ourselves who need your help and your
grace.
So we bring our prayers to you:
  for those who suffer pain;
  for those whose minds are disturbed, or have never matured;
  for those who have not had the opportunity to realize their
    potentialities;
  for those who are satisfied with something less than the life for
    which they were made;
  for those who know their guilt, their shallowness, their need, but
    who do not know of Jesus;
  for those who know that they must shortly die;
  for those who cannot wait to die.

Lord God, your Son has taken all our sufferings upon himself and
has transformed them.

Help us, who offer these prayers, to take the sufferings of others
upon ourselves, and so, by your grace, become the agents of your
transforming love.
Through Jesus Christ our Lord.

20

Lord, we have heard what you said
to the Jews and the early Christians.
Now we must talk with you
about our hopes and fears
for the Church and the world
in our own time.

We think of the Church
as your people,
Christ's body,
at least a foretaste of your new creation.
Some part of your purpose
must have been realized in it.
Sometimes the lives of Christians
do put the world to shame.
But the Church does not proclaim the Gospel so clearly
that people are left without excuse.
We cannot be surprised
when they do not find Christ easily through the Church.
How can this be put right?
How can your life be released in the Church
and transform its worship and its service?
We believe in your purpose for the Church;
help us not to be imprisoned in unbelief.

Few of us are people of great influence and responsibility,
and we wonder how our prayers can affect the course of the
world's life.

We cannot believe that war or tyranny or famine or sickness
   are the conditions under which you intend men to live.
And yet many have prayed for peace,
   but war has not been averted.
The tyrant falls
   only after he has caused much misery.
Famine is still normal for most people.
Sickness still takes its toll.
We believe that these are evils to be fought,
   and yet that mankind itself is not equipped to fight them.
We need the love only you can give,
   love which is prepared for great sacrifice,
      creative thought
      and untiring patience.
Meanwhile we ask you to give strength
      to those who suffer from these evils
   and to make us alert
      to ways of making things easier for them.

Lord, you so often astonish us
   by granting requests which were only half-formed,
   by enriching our experience in unexpected ways,
   by reminding us of factors we had overlooked.
However you answer these prayers,
   may the outcome be
      that we love you more,
      understand your purpose better,
      and believe in you with greater confidence.

21

Jacob at Bethel: Gen. 28.10-17

Heavenly Father, in our wandering we feared that we had left you
  behind, and were on our own. In emptiness we looked forward
  without hope, and thought that life had lost its meaning.
But always you are here: here is the house of God, and here is the
  gate of heaven.

22

Jacob at Peniel: Gen. 32.24-30

Heavenly Father, in seeking your kingdom give us the single mind
  of Jacob,
    that we may take life by the throat
      to shake out every ounce of meaning;
    that we may engage in deadly conflict,
      and hang on though our knuckles bleed;
to receive at last our Lord's new, proud name of 'Christian'.

23

'I have called you by name, you are mine.' Isa. 43.1-7

Almighty God, our loving heavenly Father,
    when the futility of life depresses us and we feel our nonentity,
  you have the courtesy to call us by name,
    and we know that we belong to you.
  You give us dignity
    and nothing can daunt our new-found courage.
Our thanks, through Jesus Christ, our Lord.

24

'Jesus said (to Martha, sister of Lazarus), "Did I not tell you that if you have faith you will see the glory of God?"' John 11.40

Heavenly Father, you have called us into faith, and we believe that with you everything is possible; and yet our nerve fails, and we recoil from life's crucial test.

At such fearful times encourage us to persist in faith that we may see your glory.

Through Jesus Christ, our Lord.

25

'Not a spirit of slavery . . . but a Spirit that makes us sons.' Rom. 8.15

God,
    our integrity is broken,
    our self-esteem is gone.
Life beats us down;
    we feel the power that can destroy, and we are nothing.
And yet we hear ourselves cry, 'Father!'
        Our loving heavenly Father,
            with you is sanity,
            our beginning and our life,
                our peace.

26

'You are the Christ.' Mark 8.29, etc.

Heavenly Father,
    help us like Peter
        to trust you enough to obey you;
        to follow though this will be to fail you;
        to persist, that after our humiliation we may hear you come again to bid us follow, and our faith be then of rock that Satan cannot shift.
Through Jesus Christ, our Lord.

27

'This is my beloved Son. Listen to him.' Mark 9.7, etc.

Heavenly Father,
    in Jesus, your beloved Son, you move us to adoration.
        He breaks our self-esteem.
        He grips us in our life.
        He inspires us to believe.
            In the depth of his person we see heaven open
            and for our life's sake we must listen to him.

28

'For he was teaching his disciples . . .' Mark 9.31

Heavenly Father,
    as your disciples needed to learn that between you and the kingdom was a cross,
    teach us that all those securities we had taken for granted, of health, integrity and self-confidence, must fail;
        and our heart and mind break before we begin to learn what it is to be a Christian.
Teach us how to die in our pride that we may learn to live in Christ.

29

'. . . And those who followed were afraid.' Mark 10.32

Heavenly Father,
    we have answered your call and have said that we will follow you,
    and now we are afraid that we have involved ourselves in a life that is too much for us.
Help us to a firmer resolution, to follow our Lord so closely that life shall not crowd him from sight:
and as we keep him in view
    put strength in our feet and joy in our heart.

30

'Are you able to drink the cup that I drink?' Mark 10.38

Heavenly Father,
    we have decided for your kingdom and dared to take your cup.
    But we confess that we do not understand the fearsome conse-
        quences of obedience.
When we are brought to the test steady our nerve and hold us in our
    faith;
    that we may sail through heavy seas, and ride the frightening
        storm.
Through Jesus Christ, our Lord.

Prayers for Illumination

I

Lord, all your treasures of wisdom and knowledge are hidden in
    Christ.
You reveal them to us through words spoken in his name.
May we understand and obey.

2

Lord, help us to understand what has been done for our redemption,
    so that Christ may live in our hearts by faith,
    and be proclaimed in our lives by love.

3

As we follow the story of our Lord's life on earth,
    may we become more truly his disciples.

4

Give us, Lord, a clear vision of the truth,
    faith in your power,
    and confident assurance of your love.

5

Lord, may the gospel be to us more than mere words.
May the Holy Spirit produce in us strong conviction.

6

May the God of our Lord Jesus Christ give us the wisdom and vision
    which lead to the knowledge of him.

Ascriptions of Glory

1

Now to him who is able to do immeasurably more than all we can ask or conceive, by the power which is at work among us, to him be glory in the church and in Christ Jesus from generation to generation evermore.

2

To the God of all grace, who has called us into his eternal glory in Christ, belong glory and power for ever and ever.

3

To him who can keep us from falling and set us in the presence of his glory, jubilant and above reproach, to the only God our Saviour, be glory and majesty, might and authority, through Jesus Christ our Lord, before all time, now, and in all ages to come

4

Now to the King of all worlds, immortal, invisible, the only God, be honour and glory for ever and ever.

5

To him who loves us and freed us from our sins with his life's blood, who made of us a royal house, to serve as the priests of his God and Father – to him be glory and dominion for ever and ever.

6

Praise and honour, glory and might, to him who sits on the throne
and to the Lamb for ever and ever.

(*See also 'Closing Prayers' no. 4, page 74.*)

Offering of the Collection

I

We dedicate this money, Lord, for the work of the church,
and we ask you to use all that we have and are in your service.

2

Lord, please accept the money we have given.

3

Everything in heaven and earth comes from you, Lord.
We give you only what is yours.
May you be praised for ever and ever.

4

Lord Jesus Christ, you were rich,
   yet for our sake you became poor,
      so that through your poverty we might become rich.
Accept this collection as a token of our gratitude
   for all you have done.

5

Help us who have received so freely from you
   to give as freely in our turn,
and so have the pleasure of giving
   as well as the happiness of receiving.

6

By means of these gifts, Lord, we express our longing
  that all men should acknowledge and obey you.

7

Father, every good gift comes from you.
You give generously without refusing or reproaching anyone.
May our gifts assist the preaching of the gospel,
  so that men may be remade in your likeness.

8

As we bring this offering, Father,
  we acknowledge that the money we do not bring is yours as well.
Help us to use it as may best further your purpose
  and benefit our fellow men.

9

Father, Creator, everything on earth is yours.
  We have nothing that can make you richer,
    for it all comes from you in the first place.
  But what we have we bring –
    the acknowledgment that we live thanks to you,
    and that without you we have nothing and can do nothing.

Father, Redeemer, everything on earth is doubly yours.
  Though it belonged to you in the first place,
    men treated it as theirs, refusing to recognize your rights.
  But you sent your Son to claim what ought never to have been
      denied you;
    and he paid the world's ransom with his life.

So we have not been disowned by you, or left to our fate.
    You have put paid to our fear
      alike of meeting you
      and of losing you.
By the Spirit that makes us sons, we can thankfully say,
    'Our Father . . .'[1]

10

Father, we give back to you in thankfulness what you have given to
    us in your kindness.
We acknowledge that the world and its resources are not ours but
    yours, and that you have put us in charge as your trustees.
Help us to exercise responsibly the authority you give us in your
    world.
Let Jesus your Son be the pattern for all our dealings with one
    another, and with the rest of creation.
      He is truth: so help us to take our quest for truth seriously,
        whether in the research laboratories, or in the dialectic of
        philosophy and politics.
      He is life: so give us reverence for life, whether on the poultry-
        farms or on the roads.
Yet with his care give us also his joy in life.
With his compassion give us also his strength.
      So that in everything he may be everything to us.
Praise and victory be to him from all, and in all, for ever and ever.

11

In this prayer, after the words, 'In the name of Jesus Christ', *all say
together,* 'We bring them to you'.

Lord God, with these gifts we offer you our lives
    to do your work in the world.

[1] See p. 139 for a modern translation of the Lord's Prayer.

Father, take our bodies and our minds:
　　In the name of Jesus Christ
　　All: We bring them to you.

Father, take our family life,
　our friendships,
　our relationships with other people:
　　In the name of Jesus Christ
　　All: We bring them to you.

Father, take our work and our leisure:
　　In the name of Jesus Christ
　　All: We bring them to you.

Father, take our conversations with other people
　and our conversations about other people:
　　In the name of Jesus Christ
　　All: We bring them to you.

Father, take our ambitions and our plans for the future:
　　In the name of Jesus Christ
　　All: We bring them to you.

12

Eternal God, Father of our Lord Jesus Christ,
we bring you these gifts because we know
that our life and all human life
rightfully belongs to you
and that everything we have we hold in trust from you.

We praise you for everything you have done for mankind in Jesus
　　Christ.
Help us, through him, to make our own offering complete
　by living in obedience to you.

And hear us, through him, as we pray for the world
which belongs to you, but does not know you.

(*Appropriate intercessions may be used at this point*)

> Eternal God,
>> because of what you have done in Jesus Christ
>> we know that in spite of all that is wrong in it
>> this world belongs to you.
> Help us, and all Christ's people,
>> to live and speak the good news of your love
>> so that all human life
>> – our life and every man's life –
>> can be an offering to you.
> We ask it in his name.

13

At the Lord's Supper

P 48.

Holy Father, Creator, Redeemer and King,
We set before you this money, this bread and this wine.
They represent the work you have given us to do
  and the ability you have given us with which to do it.
We bring them to express our longing that all our work and life may
  be an offering to you.
Use them, therefore, we pray, to bring us to the joy of communion
  with Jesus Christ,
both here among your people, and when we have dispersed to
  serve you in the world.

14

At the Lord's Supper

Lord God,
we bring to you the ordinary things of life –   Latham.
    food and drink and money –
and in bringing them we bring ourselves.

Take us and our gifts of money
    to do your work in the world.
Take this food and drink
    from our tables to your table
    and feed us with your love.

Through Jesus Christ our Lord.

15

At the Lord's Supper

Father, accept our offering.

Not ours but yours this bread,
    lest we forget that life is more than food.
Not ours but yours this wine,
    lest we look for our enjoyment in pleasures of a moment
    and drown the voice of him who alone can bid us be of good cheer.
Not ours but yours this money, this purchasing-power,
    earned by the skill of hand and brain,
    lest we forget that we are not our own
    and refuse to serve you with the strength you have given.

Living God, give us bread that will satisfy our hunger
    and nourish the life of mankind.

Give us mirth that will carry us through the sleep of death
  to an awakening with no bitter taste in the mouth.
Use our money to buy the imperishable goods
  of love and mercy and peace.

And take our hands to do your work,
  our work to serve you in the world.

Through Jesus Christ our Lord.

Closing Prayers

1

Lord Jesus, Word of the Father,
    spoken in mercy and power to mankind,
    may all power serve you, all mercy follow your lead.

Word of pity,
    let men find in you an example to inspire them without daunting
        them,
    and a love to reassure them without smothering them.

Word of life,
    let men find in you the key to all the riddles of existence,
    and the door to an eternal hope.

Word of command,
    may we go now, refreshed by your presence,
    and put your plans into action and your energy to good use.

For your name's sake.

2

Lord God, you have come near to us and shown us
    something of your patience,
    something of your sympathy,
    something of your love.

Give us, Lord, as we go about our life in the world,
    patience when men are indifferent to your claims,
    sympathy for the needs of all your creatures,
    a love which reflects your forgiving love for men.

Through Jesus Christ our Lord.

3

We have seen the true light,
  we have received the bread of life,
  we have found the true revelation of God,
  we worship him, Father, Son and Holy Spirit.
May our mouths now and always be filled with his praise.

4

To you, Lord Jesus; to you, our heavenly Father;
  to you, most real and holy Spirit;
    let all the world give thanks.
For what you have done in time past;
  for what your love is doing now, in our own days;
  for what you will do in time to come;
    let all the world give thanks.
Glory to you for ever and ever.

5

After the Lord's Supper

Holy Father, we thank you for making your home among us
  and revealing to us the knowledge, faith and indestructible life
    that come through Jesus, your Son.
As you have given mankind food and drink for our enjoyment,
  so you have given us, through your Son,
    the nourishment of your Holy Spirit and enduring life.
Deliver your Church from every evil
  and teach it to love you perfectly.
As bread like this was once scattered over the fields
  and gathered together to become one,
    so gather your people from the four winds into one Church.
To you be glory for ever.

6

After the Lord's Supper

For the bread that we have eaten
For the wine that we have tasted
For the life that you have given:
    Father, Son and Holy Spirit,
    We will praise you.

For the life of Christ within us
Turning all our fears to freedom
Helping us to live for others:
    Father, Son and Holy Spirit,
    We will praise you.

For the strength of Christ to lead us
In our living and our dying,
In the end with all your people
    Father, Son and Holy Spirit,
    We will praise you.

Blessings and Dismissals

I

The grace of the Lord Jesus Christ, and the love of God, and fellowship in the Holy Spirit, be with you all.

2

May the Lord of peace himself give you peace at all times, wherever you may be. The Lord be with you all.

3

May the peace of God, which is beyond our utmost understanding (*or*, of far more worth than human reasoning), keep guard over your hearts and thoughts, in Christ Jesus our Lord.

4

May the Lord bless you and protect you.
May the Lord smile on you and show you his favour.
May the Lord befriend you and prosper you.

5

May the God of peace, who brought up from the dead our Lord Jesus, the great Shepherd of the sheep, by the blood of the eternal covenant, make you perfect in all goodness so that you may do his will, and may he make of us what he would have us be through Jesus Christ, to whom be glory for ever and ever.

6

May God, the giver of hope, fill you with all joy and peace because you trust in him, so that you may have abundant hope through the power of the Holy Spirit.

7

Go out into the world in peace. Be brave; keep hold of what is good; never pay back wrong for wrong; encourage the faint-hearted; support the weak and the distressed; give due honour to everyone. Be always joyful; pray continually; give thanks whatever happens; for this is what God in Christ wills for you.

8

Jesus said: 'Peace I leave with you: my own peace I give to you. It is not as the world gives its greetings that I give you peace. Set your troubled hearts at rest, and banish your fears.'
Peace to you all who belong to Christ.

PART II

Sacraments and Ordinances

Order for the Lord's Supper

After praise and prayer, reading and preaching, the minister continues either as under [A] *or as under* [B]:

[A]

Lift up your hearts.
People: We lift them up unto the Lord.
Let us give thanks unto our Lord God.
People: It is meet and right so to do.
It is very meet, right, and our bounden duty, that we should at all times, and in all places, give thanks unto thee, O Lord, holy Father, almighty, everlasting God.
(*Here a proper Preface may be included*)
Therefore with angels and archangels, and with all the company of heaven, we laud and magnify thy glorious name; evermore praising thee and saying,
All: Holy, holy, holy Lord God of hosts,
Heaven and earth are full of thy glory:
Glory be to thee, O Lord most high.

(Let us pray.)

We give you thanks and praise, our Father, for all that you have done for the world.
We must not take even our existence for granted:
it is your love which has given us life.
(*Here particular thanksgivings may be inserted as appropriate*)
But even more we must praise you for our Lord Jesus Christ:
because he was born in Bethlehem and brought up in Nazareth;
because he went about Galilee healing the sick and preaching the good news of the kingdom;

CPPW F

because when he taught, people heard him gladly yet were
astonished at his authority;
because he called and trained disciples;
because he set his face resolutely towards Jerusalem, and gave his
life a ransom for many;
because he showed himself to his disciples after his death.

or

because he became man, and came to live among us;
because it was meat and drink for him to do your will and finish
your work;
because he revealed in words what he had learned from you;
because he died to gather your scattered children;
because he not only laid down his life but took it again.

or

because you have exalted him and made him our Lord;
because in him you have proved your love towards us;
because in him you were reconciling the world to yourself;
because in him you have confirmed and fulfilled all your promises.

We praise you for the new covenant sealed by his blood, for the
forgiveness of our sins and the gift of a new life.

We therefore set before you this bread and this cup, as the thank-
offering of your people; and we thank you that in your fatherly
mercy, by our Lord's provision, and with the help of the Holy
Spirit, it may be the means by which we remember his holy
sacrifice and share his body and blood.

And Jesus has given us the confidence and the longing to offer you
ourselves a living sacrifice, dedicated and fit for your acceptance.
May your kingdom come and your will be done in and through us
all.

[B]

Lift up your hearts.
People: We lift them up to the Lord.
Let us give thanks to the Lord our God.
People: It is right that we should.

(Let us pray.)

It is our duty and our delight, Lord God our Father, to give you
thanks and praise for all that you have done for the world. Our
hearts are full of gratitude to you, because you loved the world
so much that you gave your only Son, so that everyone who has
faith in him may not die but have eternal life.

We thank you that Jesus was born among us; that he lived our
common life on earth; that he suffered and died for us; that he
rose again; and that he is always present through the Holy Spirit.

Remembering these things, we celebrate once again the supper of
the Lord. We pray that despite our sins and doubts the Holy
Spirit may transform what we are doing, so that as we eat the
bread and drink the wine we may share in the eternal life of Christ.

We thank you that we do not celebrate this supper alone, but in
company with all your people, past, present and to come. With
them and all creation we praise you and say: give you our thanks.
All: Holy, holy, holy,   Amen.
      Mighty Lord God,
      Everything makes your greatness known:
      We acknowledge it too.

The Communion follows, the minister saying:

The Lord Jesus, on the night of his arrest, took bread, and when he
had given thanks he broke it and said: This is my body, which is
for you; do this in remembrance of me.

The bread is distributed, and the congregation may be invited to partake with one of the following sentences:

(1) Take this and eat it: this is the body of Christ, which is broken for you. Do this in remembrance of him.

(2) When we break the bread, is it not a means of sharing in the body of Christ? Because there is one loaf, we, many as we are, are one body; for it is one loaf of which we all partake.

(3) The body of our Lord Jesus Christ, the bread of life.

(4) Take and eat this in remembrance that Christ died for you, and feed on him in your heart by faith with thanksgiving.

Now (or before the bread is distributed) the minister says:

In the same way Jesus took the cup after supper, and said:
This cup is the new covenant sealed by my blood. Whenever you drink it, do this in remembrance of me.

The wine is distributed, and the congregation may be invited to partake with one of the following sentences:

(1) This cup is the new covenant sealed by Christ's blood, which was shed so that the sins of many might be forgiven. Drink from it.

(2) When we bless the cup of blessing, is it not a means of sharing in the blood of Christ?

(3) The blood of our Lord Jesus Christ, the true vine.

(4) Drink this in remembrance that Christ's blood was shed for you, and be thankful.

When all have partaken, prayer is offered, as follows or as on pages 73-75:

Lord God
we praise and worship and adore you
for the food we have received at this table.

You have sent your Holy Spirit among us
   to make our eating and drinking here
   a memorial of our Lord Jesus Christ.
May your Spirit help us tomorrow
   to make our living and working,
      our loving and doing and thinking,
   a memorial of him:
so that in the end, with the great company of the redeemed,
   we may eat and drink and be glad with him
   in the glory of the eternal kingdom.

To him, with you our Father and the Holy Spirit, one God,
   may all that lives and breathes,
      the world and all creation,
   give glory, worship and praise,
   now and for ever.

Additional Material for the Lord's Supper

I

After 'Sursum corda' (ending with the people's response, 'It is meet and right so to do', or, 'It is right that we should').

Yes, it is right, only right, the only thing which is always and everywhere right, that we men should give thanks to you our God, the
   source of all being, the controller of the process of creation, the
   matchless and tireless director of operations for our rescue and
   rehabilitation.

From the first you began to call men your people, your family, your
   children.
You brought them out of slavery into freedom.
You gave them bread from heaven to eat.
You sprang water for them from the flinty rock.

Your presence was like a bright cloud overshadowing them –
   like smoke on the mountain for Moses the Lawgiver,
   like smoke in the temple for Isaiah the prophet –
too much for mortal eyes and unclean lips:
   yet the face shone which had approached that brightness,
   and the voice rang clear for truth which had cried, 'Woe is me'.

And you are the same, yesterday, today and for ever.
High and lifted up, you yet have your dwelling among men,
   and are making all things new through the man you have appointed;
   Jesus Christ, in whom the Law and the prophets are complete.

In him you stand plainly revealed as our heavenly Father,
   and we as your family and household.

In him you have rescued us from the power of darkness,
  and have brought us into the light of your promise.
In him you give us the bread of life,
  and an inner spring always welling up for eternal life.

Like a bright cloud you overshadowed his baptism.
Under the same token of your presence he was transfigured on the
  mountain.
And now, beyond death, your glory has received him out of our sight,
  whereby we know that his forgiveness is your forgiveness,
    his attitude towards men once is your attitude towards men eter-
      nally.

Father, we all have sinned and fall short of your glory.
Have mercy upon us.
Burn out the evil in us and make us your messengers:
  let our faces glow with your presence wherever we go,
  and our voices ring clear for truth whether it is popular or not.

Through Jesus Christ our Lord.

2

After 'Sursum corda'

It is fitting that rational creatures
  should continually and in every way
  acknowledge their maker
  and fulfil the purpose for which he created them.
But we have special reason for doing this,
  because we believe in the gospel of Jesus Christ.
We believe
  that the life of ancient Israel prepared for his coming;
we believe
  that his life was not only the effort and achievement of a man
    but the presence and action of God.

We believe
  that he achieved the full stature of manhood;
  that he defeated the pressure of sin at its strongest;
  that because he has been raised from the dead
  and has power to give himself by the Holy Spirit,
  he brings the deliverance of God
    to all who trust in him.

Thank you, Lord God,
  for your generous provision for your world in Jesus Christ.

Remembering this,
  we celebrate this supper once again.
As we eat and drink,
  do for us all that you have promised.
Allow us to share in the life so generously given to the world.
And may all men come to know you through Jesus Christ.

NOTE *The anamnesis in this prayer is based on the paragraph 'Christian awareness of God' in the Congregational Union of England and Wales' 'A Declaration of Faith' (First provisional draft, 1964, p. 11).*

3

After 'Sursum corda'

God the Father, you are worthy of praise
  because you are the Lord of the whole universe,
  because you have given us the earth's resources,
  because we are able to think and plan and worship,
  because Jesus has opened the way for us to think your thoughts,
    to co-operate with your plan, and to worship you alone.

God the Son, you are worthy of praise
  because you are the Lord of the Church,
  because in the Church you are calling us to share in your mission
    to the world,
  because as an assurance of your presence with us to the end of
    time you have given us this sacrament of your body and blood.

God the Holy Spirit, you are worthy of praise
  because you are the Lord of our life,
  because you impel us to offer ourselves in worship,
    and empower us to serve and bear our witness,
  because you use the bread and the wine, so that they may become
    for us the body and blood of Christ,
  because you are in us, and help us to grow into that fulness of life
    for which we were created.

*The prayer may end with an ascription of glory to the Trinity, or may
lead thence into the saying of the 'Sanctus'.*

4

After 'Sursum corda'
In this prayer, to the words, 'Our thanksgiving will never cease', *the
response is,* 'Our praise will never end'.

It is indeed right, and always right
to thank you and praise you, eternal and loving God.

  For the joys of human life,
    for the wonder of loving another person and being loved,
    for friendship and family life,
    (and especially today for . . . .),
      our thanksgiving will never cease,
      People: Our praise will never end.

For the wonders of your creation –
    the earth spinning in darkness round the sun,
    the stars scattered in the depths of space –
and for the teeming life on earth;
for the long story of change and growth
    from the mud in the dark depths of ocean
    to the mind and power of man:
(and especially today for . . . .);
      our thanksgiving will never cease,
      People: Our praise will never end.

*The prayer continues with one of the three paragraphs following, or
with material adapted from the prayer on page 33 f.*

(1) But most of all we praise you for the wonder of your love.
    You are the eternal God,
      Lord of space and time,
      maker and master of us all:
    yet you have opened your heart to us in Jesus Christ
      so that we have seen your very self
      fully revealed
      – in the helpless dependence of a baby
      – in the muscle and bone and mind of a man
      – in the growth and work of a human life
      – in the humiliation and pain of death on a cross
      – and in the glory that changed death into life
        in the silence of an empty tomb.
    Eternal God, because you have shown yourself to us
      and loved us in Jesus Christ,
        our thanksgiving will never cease,
        People: Our praise will never end.

(2) But most of all, eternal God, we praise and adore you
    for everything you have done for mankind in Jesus Christ.
Because he was born as one of us and shared our human life,
because on the cross he won the victory over evil and death,

because he was raised from death
and lives for ever with us by the Holy Spirit,
our thanksgiving will never cease,
People: Our praise will never end.

(3) But most of all, eternal God, we praise and adore you
for everything you have done for mankind in Jesus Christ.
Because he lived as one of us
and everything he did reflected your love,
because he met the full force of the evil that drags us down
but never gave in to it,
because he lived his whole life in loving obedience to you
even though the road of obedience led to the cross,
because you brought him back from death
to be the Lord of living and dead,
our thanksgiving will never cease,
People: Our praise will never end.

After these or similar thanksgivings, the prayer ends as follows:
Remembering this, we celebrate the supper of our Lord Jesus Christ.
And as on the night of his arrest he took bread and a cup
and after giving thanks to you
shared them with his disciples and said:
'Do this as a memorial of me',
so now we give thanks to you
by sharing this bread and this cup.

As we eat and drink together
we ask that by the Holy Spirit's power
Christ who died for us may live in us
so that we may live for him.

And now, with all creation
and in company with all your people
past, present, and to come,

we worship and adore you, eternal God,
   for ever praising you and saying,
All: Holy, holy, holy . . . . *etc.*

(*Alternative translations of the 'Sanctus' are on pages 81-83.*)

5

After 'Sursum corda'

It is proper and good for us
   always and everywhere
   to give you our thanks,
   God and Father of our Lord Jesus Christ.

We thank you for life, for memory and hope.
We thank you for growth, for certainty and change.
We thank you for all our powers to reason and imagine.

But most of all we thank you for your love to us and our access to
   you,
For the Holy Spirit joining us to you and each other,
And for Jesus our Lord . . .

either

   . . . who is light to the world,
   true bread from heaven,
   the way and the truth and life.

or

   . . . whom you lifted from death when he had finished your work,
   who embodied your purpose,
   is nearest your heart,
   uniquely your Son since before things began.

Because he called men his friends,
   and made himself a sacrifice for them,
   and broke the bread with them and shared the cup,
   giving thanks to you and saying,
      'This is my body,
      This is my covenant blood',
so now we break bread and share wine,
   asking you to blend your action with ours
   so that we may be united with Christ,
      may share his worship,
      gain his life,
      and go out to be his body in the world.

Father, we praise you.
With all who adore you we join to give glory,
   to praise you for ever and ever in saying . . .

(All join in saying the 'Sanctus'.)

NOTE   *For opening prayers, see p. 17 ff. (especially nos. 19-20).*
For the offering of the collection, see p. 66 ff. (especially nos. 13-15).
For closing prayers, see p. 73 ff. (especially nos. 2, 3, 5 and 6).

Order for Baptism

NOTE *This order is intended to be used for both the baptism of infants and the baptism of believers. Those parts of the service which pertain only to believers are to be found in the left-hand column; material pertaining only to infants is placed in the right-hand column.*

p29 then

Lesson. Mark 1 v 1 –11 (TEV)

At the appropriate point in the service the minister says:

We are now going to administer the sacrament of baptism
to M.N. to

We have come together, this evening the son/daughter of Mr and
so that you may receive the Sacrament Mrs N.
of Baptism.

What does this mean?

After his resurrection Jesus said to the disciples: 'Full authority in heaven and on earth has been committed to me. Go forth therefore and ~~make all nations my disciples~~: baptize ~~men~~ *people* everywhere in the name of the Father and the Son and the Holy Spirit, ~~and teach them~~ to ~~observe all that I have commanded you.~~ And be assured, I am *A moment ago* with you always, to the end of time.' (Matt. 28.18-20 NEB) *we read of Jesus* — *from the very earliest days of the Church.* *We might also* Therefore, when people became Christians, they were baptized. *read that on the* That is, they went down under water and came up again. This *day of Pentecost,* meant that they were dying to their old way of life, and rising again *Peter* to a new way of life. Jesus had made this possible by his own death and resurrection. *Although this evening we will use only a little water* ~~Although for~~ the most part the Church ~~no longer baptizes by immersion in water,~~ the meaning of baptism is still the same. It stands for the new beginning God has given us through Jesus. It shows that we are to live as God's ~~children~~ *people* in his family, the Church. It declares that God gives us the Holy Spirit as the guarantee of eternal life.

Tonight ~~Today~~, God our Father calls M.N. by name to enter *into* this inheritance.

But first, I require you to make

~~Let us hear from *him* *his*~~ profession of faith, and ~~*his*~~ declaration that *he* intends, with God's *your* help, to live as a Christian.

children

But since ~~a~~ little child cannot understand this at the time, *his their* parents and the Church must promise to bring *him* up in the Christian faith, so that *he* has every opportunity to confirm and complete *his* baptism by choosing for *~~himself~~ themselves* to follow Christ and to serve him as a member of his Church.

M.N., in presenting yourself for baptism, do you confess with us your faith in Jesus Christ as Saviour and Lord; and do you *your* promise, relying on God's grace, to follow Christ and to serve him all your life in the fellowship of the Church?
Answer: I do.

Do you promise to share with us in the duties of membership in this church, in worship and in Church Meeting in giving and in service?
Answer: I do.

May God bless you & give you grace faithfully to fulfil these promises.
Let us pray

Mr and Mrs N., you have brought your son/daughter for baptism: Do you confess with us your faith in Jesus Christ as Saviour and Lord?
Answer: We do.

Do you promise, relying on God's help, to bring your son/daughter up in the Christian faith?
Answer: We do.

(*To the congregation*:)
Do you, the members of this *congregation* ~~church~~, promise to play your part in the Christian upbringing of th~~is~~*ese* child~~~~*ren*? *In acceptance of* *Answer*: We do. *this responsibility, I invite you to stand.*

M.N., I baptize you in the name of the Father and the Son and the Holy Spirit. "*The Lord bless you & keep you . . —*"

May God fill you with joy and peace through your faith in him.

May the Lord bless you and protect you.

As God has called you, live up to your calling. Never be ashamed of your testimony to our Lord. Amen.

And may God fill you with joy + peace as you faith in him.

Start

M.N., in the name of the Lord Jesus Christ, I declare that you have been received into membership of the Church by baptism. We, the members of this congregation, welcome you as a partner in the common life of this church, and promise you our friendship and our prayers. *Here the minister (with other representatives of the church) shakes hands with the new member.*

May the Lord smile on you and show you his favour.
May the Lord befriend you and prosper you. Amen.

I declare that M.N. has been received into the Church by baptism. May God help us all to keep our promises. Jesus said: 'Whoever receives one such child in my name, receives me.'

Let us pray.

Lord God, we give you praise for all that you have done for us.

For every good influence - - - -

We thank you especially today for calling M.N. by baptism into membership of the Church. May *he* never cease to wonder at what you have done for *him*. Help *him* to continue firmly in the Christian faith, to bear witness to your love, and to let the Spirit mould *his* character and conduct.

We ask that you will make the baptism of all of us real and complete, so that we may live together in the joy and power of the Holy Spirit, and at the last

We thank you especially today for declaring your love for this *them* child before *he* can even hear about you. As you have loved *him them* from the beginning, so continue to protect and guide *him*. *them* May *he they* become a loyal disciple*s* of Jesus. Help *his their* father*s* and mother*s* and us, the members of this church, to keep the promises we have made.

We thank you for your goodness to these parents, for the wonder of new life, for the enrichment of their home. Help

live for ever in your presence: through Jesus Christ our Lord.

all parents to give their children security and freedom, and by their love to show the meaning of your love.

Whether we are young or old, we ask together that you will make our baptism real and complete, so that we may live together in the joy and power of the Holy Spirit, and at the last live for ever in your presence, through Jesus Christ our Lord.

CPPW G

Order for Confirmation of Baptism
or
Admission to Church Membership

At the appropriate point in the service, the minister says:

We are now to receive M.N. into full membership of the Church.
When *he* was baptized, God claimed *him* as his own, and *he* was received into the Church. *He* now comes to confirm what was done in baptism, to confess *his* faith in the Lord Jesus and to offer *himself* to God as his willing servant. *He* also seeks to covenant with us in membership of this church and of the whole Church of God.

Let us hear from *him* a declaration of *his* faith and intention.

M.N., do you confess with us your faith in Jesus Christ as Saviour and Lord; and do you promise, relying on God's grace, to follow Christ and serve him all your life in the fellowship of the Church?
Answer: I do.

Do you promise to share with us in the duties of membership in this church, in worship and in Church Meeting, in giving and in service?
Answer: I do.

I declare that you have been received into full membership of the Church of God on confession of faith. We, the members of this congregation, receive you as a partner in the common life of this church, and promise you our friendship and our prayers. In the name of the Lord Jesus Christ I/we welcome you.

Here the minister (with other representatives of the church) shakes hands with the new member.

Let us pray.

Lord God, we give you thanks for all the ways in which you have brought M.N. to yourself. May *he* never cease to wonder at what you have done for *him*. Help *him* to continue firmly in the Christian faith, to bear witness to your love, and to let the Spirit mould *his* character and conduct.

We ask that you will make the membership of all of us real and complete, so that we may live together in the joy and power of your Holy Spirit and at the last live for ever in your presence: through Jesus Christ our Lord.

NOTE *For other appropriate prayers, see 'Supplication and Intercession', nos. 4 and 5 (pp. 46 and 47).*

Order for Christian Marriage

NOTE   *In order to comply with the Marriage Acts, 1949 to 1960, the traditional and archaic wording of the Declaration of no Impediment and the first part of the Vows has had to be retained. For the sake of uniformity of style the pronoun 'thee' has also been retained at the end of the Vows.*

The couple to be married stand together, the woman on the left hand of the man. The service may begin with a hymn. Then the minister says:

The Declaration of Purpose

We have come together in God's presence and as his congregation so that A.B. and C.D. may be joined in Christian marriage.

Marriage, like our creation as male and female, owes its existence to God, who intends that husband and wife should love each other, and be faithful to each other throughout their life, and that children should be born and brought up surrounded by love and be given the instruction and correction which belong to a Christian upbringing.

Such marriage must not be entered into lightly or thoughtlessly, but with mutual respect, with reverence for God, and with the intention to obey his will: then we can be assured that God will give us his joy and peace.

A.B. and C.D. seek such Christian marriage. If anyone knows that they cannot be legally married, he should say so now. (*To the couple*:) And you also must say that you know of no reason why you may not be legally married.

The Declaration that there is no Impediment

The man says after the minister:

I do solemnly declare that I know not of any lawful impediment why I, (*full name*), may not be joined in matrimony to (*full name*).

Then the woman says after the minister:

I do solemnly declare that I know not of any lawful impediment why I, (*full name*), may not be joined in matrimony to (*full name*).

The Question

The minister then says to the man:

A.B., will you take C.D. as your wife in Christian marriage? Will you love her, comfort her, honour and keep her, in sickness and in health, and be faithful to her as long as you both live?

The man answers: I will.

The minister then says to the woman:

C.D., will you take A.B. as your husband in Christian marriage? Will you love him, comfort him, honour and keep him, in sickness and in health, and be faithful to him as long as you both live?

The woman answers: I will.

Prayer for sincerity in making the Marriage Vows

The minister may use the following:

Eternal God, true and loving Father, we ask you to help A. and C. as they enter their marriage. Make them as conscious of your presence as they are of ours, and give them the confidence that you will help them to be true to each other, through Jesus Christ our Lord.

Here, if desired, may follow the Giving Away, when the minister says: 'Who gives the bride away?' (or: 'Who gives this woman to be married to this man?'), to which may be made the response: 'I do'.

The Vows

The man and woman turn and face each other. Then the man with his right hand takes the woman by her right hand and says after the minister:

I call upon these persons here present to witness that I, A.B. (*full name*), do take thee, C.D. (*full name*) to be my lawful wedded wife, in accordance with God's holy will, to have and to hold from this day forward, for better for worse, for richer for poorer, in sickness and in health, to love and to cherish until death parts us, and to this end I pledge thee my word.

They then loose hands, and the woman with her right hand takes the man by his right hand, and says after the minister:

I call upon these persons here present to witness that I, C.D. (*full name*), do take thee, A.B. (*full name*), to be my lawful wedded husband, in accordance with God's holy will, to have and to hold from this day forward, for better for worse, for richer for poorer, in sickness and in health, to love and to cherish until death parts us, and to this end I pledge thee my word.

The Giving of the Ring

The man places a ring on the fourth finger of the woman's left hand and says after the minister:

I give you this ring in God's name as a symbol of all that we shall share.

If desired, the woman may then place a ring on the fourth finger of the man's left hand, saying the same words.

The Declaration of Marriage

The minister then says:

A.B. and C.D. have declared before God and this congregation that they will live together in Christian marriage; they have made sacred promises to each other; and they have symbolized it by joining hands and by giving and receiving a ring (*or* by exchanging rings). I therefore pronounce them to be husband and wife, in the name of God, the Father, the Son and the Holy Spirit. What God has joined together, man must not separate.

The Blessing

The minister says:

May the Lord bless you and protect you.
May the Lord smile on you and show you his favour.
May the Lord befriend you and prosper you.

There follow (after a hymn or psalm, if desired) a reading from the Bible, a short address, and prayers such as these:

Eternal God, Creator and Father of us all –

We praise you for creating mankind male and female, so that each may find fulfilment in the other.

We praise you for all the ways in which your love comes into our lives, and for all the joys that can come to men and women through marriage.

Today especially we think of A. and C., as they begin their life together.

With them we thank you for giving them life, and for bringing them together in marriage.

With them we thank you for the love and care of their parents, which has guided them to maturity and prepared them for each other.

With them we pray for their parents, that at this moment of parting they may find new happiness as they share their children's joy.

And now, Father, we pray for A. and C. themselves.

Give them the strength to keep the vows they have made, to be loyal and faithful to each other, and to support each other throughout their life; may they bear each other's burdens and share each other's joys.

Help them to be honest and patient with each other, to be loving and wise parents of any children they have, and to welcome both friends and strangers into their home.

In all their future together, may they enjoy each other's lives and grow through each other's love.

Finally, we ask you to keep them faithful to you, and at the end of this life on earth to receive them, and us, into your eternal kingdom, through Jesus Christ.

To him, with you our Father and the Holy Spirit, one God, may honour and praise be given, now and for ever.

A hymn may be sung, after which the minister pronounces a general blessing.

Order for Burial or Cremation

The minister says:
Blessed are those who mourn, for they shall be comforted.

Jesus said: I am the resurrection and I am life. If a man has faith in me, even though he die, he shall come to life; and no one who is alive and has faith shall ever die.

God loved the world so much that he gave his only Son, that everyone who has faith in him may not die but have eternal life.

Praise be to the God and Father of our Lord Jesus Christ who in his mercy gave us new birth into a living hope through the resurrection of Jesus Christ from the dead! The inheritance to which we are born is one that nothing can destroy or spoil or wither.

None of us lives to himself, and none of us dies to himself. At every turn life links us to the Lord, and when we die we come face to face with him. In life or death we are in the hands of the Lord. Christ lived and died and lives again to establish his lordship over dead and living.

Now we see only puzzling reflections in a mirror; but then we shall see face to face. Our knowledge now is partial; then it will be whole, like God's knowledge of us.

There is nothing in death or life, in the world as it is or the world as it shall be, nothing in all creation that can separate us from the love of God in Christ Jesus our Lord.

*One of these prayers of invocation may be offered, before or after which
a hymn may be sung.*

Father, your love is stronger than death:
  by you we are all being brought to life.
Help us, as we hear your promises,
  to believe them and receive the comfort they offer.
You are the giver of hope:
  fill us with joy and peace in believing,
  so that we may have abundant hope through the power of the Holy
    Spirit.
Glory to you, our God, for ever.

   or this

God our Father, you are a refuge and strength for us,
  a helper close at hand in time of distress.
We ask you to help us now so to hear the words of our faith
  that our fears are dispelled,
  our loneliness is eased
  and our hope reawakened.
May the Holy Spirit lift us above our natural sorrow,
  to the peace and the light of your constant love,
  in the calm eternity where you live for ever.

*Here a Psalm may be said by the congregation together, or responsively,
(or sung, if there is no hymn). Psalms 23, 39, 90 and 103 will be found
suitable. A passage from the New Testament is then read, such as one
of the following: John 14.1-6, 18-19, 27; I Corinthians 15 (selected
verses); I Peter 1.3-9; Revelation 7.9-17; 21.1-4, and 22.1-5. An
address may be given, after which prayer is offered, such as one of the
following:*

Lord God, with your whole Church we offer you our thanks and
  praise for all you have done for mankind through Jesus Christ.

By giving him to live and die for us,
  you have disclosed your gracious plan for the world
  and shown that your love has no limit:
and by raising him from the dead,
  you have promised that those who trust in him
  will share his resurrection-life.

For the assurance and hope of our faith,
and for the saints whom you have received into your eternal joy,
  we thank you, heavenly Father.
And especially now we lift up our hearts in gratitude
  for the life of N., our *brother*, now gone from among us;
  for all your goodness to *him* (through many days);
  for all that *he* was to those who loved *him*,
  and for everything in *his* life that reflected your goodness and love.
And now we bless you that *his* sins are forgiven,
  all suffering and bitterness are past and forgotten,
  and *he* is reunited with *his* dear ones who went before *him*.
Help us to be content to release *him* to you, our Father.
Assure us that in your keeping *he* is safe, and happy, and complete.
Surround us and all who mourn today with your continuing compassion.
Do not let grief overwhelm your children,
  or be unending,
  or turn them against you.
May we travel on more serenely because of today;
  and with our course charted for us by the whole company of the redeemed
  may we come at last, in the fellowship of your people,
  to the harbour where we long to be.
Through Jesus Christ our Lord.

or this

Let us give thanks to God for all that he has done for the world
  through Jesus Christ, and especially that for so many people the

bitterness and fear of death have been taken away by their faith in him;

Let us thank God for N.'s life, each of us recalling what *he* has meant to us;

Let us commit *him* to God's sure keeping;

Let us pray for the family (*or*, for those who mourn *him* most), that they may be comforted in their sorrow;

Let us remember others who mourn today;

Let us pray for ourselves, that we may be instruments of God's help to those in trouble, and that we may so live that we may not be afraid to die.

or this

Heavenly Father,
   on this sad and proud day we look to you in hope.
We dare to trust you alone.
Help us to be content to release N. to you.
Help us to believe that death is a gateway to what cannot be a lesser life;
   assure us that *he* is safe in your keeping.
Spare us from the selfishness of living in the past,
   and the luxury of private grief.
Rather, teach us to live out our lives gently with others,
   and to trust that *he* will never be far from us
   till the day when we all stand together before you.
Through Jesus Christ, our Lord.

The Lord's Prayer may be said.

Where the committal is to be in another place, this part of the service may end with a hymn and a blessing or ascription of glory.

At the place of committal, all stand.

When the earlier part of the service has been held elsewhere, the following sentence, or other similar, may be said.

The Lord says: Do not be afraid. I am the first and the last, and I am the living one: for I was dead and now I am alive for evermore.

The minister says (having previously warned the attendant and/or organist that the committal does not begin with the word 'Forasmuch'):

Seeing that the earthly life of our *brother* has come to an end, we commit *his* body to be buried (cremated),[1] confident of the resurrection to eternal life through our Lord Jesus Christ.

At a crematorium, the following sentence, or other similar, may be said while the coffin is disappearing.

They shall never again feel hunger or thirst, the sun shall not beat on them nor any scorching heat, because the Lamb who is at the heart of the throne will be their shepherd and will guide them to the springs of the water of life; and God will wipe all tears from their eyes.

A prayer follows, such as this:

God of peace, you brought back from the dead our Lord Jesus, the great shepherd of the sheep, by the blood of the eternal covenant.
   Show us the peace we should seek,
   show us the peace we must try to give,
   show us the peace we may keep,
   show us the peace you have given,
and make us what you want us to be: through Jesus Christ, to whom be glory for ever.

May the peace of God, which is beyond our utmost understanding and of far more worth than human reasoning, keep guard over your hearts and thoughts, in Christ Jesus our Lord.

[1] The words '(Earth to earth), ashes to ashes, dust to dust' may be added here.

PART III

Prayers for the Christian Year

Advent

1

Lord God, we adore you because you have come to us in the past.
  You have spoken to us in the Law of Israel.
  You have challenged us in the words of the prophets.
  You have shown us in Jesus what you are really like.

Lord God, we adore you because you still come to us now.
  You come to us through other people and their love and concern
    for us.
  You come to us through men and women who need our help.
  You come to us as we worship you with your people.

Lord God, we adore you because you will come to us at the end.
  You will be with us at the hour of death.
  You will still reign supreme when all human institutions fail.
  You will still be God when our history has run its course.

We welcome you, the God who comes.
Come to us now in the power of Jesus Christ our Lord.

2

We greet your coming, God, with wonder:
  You come to be with us; yet you remain far greater than we can
    imagine.
  You are near; yet your wisdom sets you apart from us.
  You appear among us; yet we cannot describe your glory.

We greet your coming, God, with repentance:
  We are more or less satisfied with ourselves; but your
    presence exposes our sin and failure.

We are self-confident; but you challenge our
confidence in ourselves.
We are proud of our understanding; but you show us
that we do not know everything.

We greet your coming, God, with joy:
We had no true idea of what you are like; but you
have shown us yourself in Jesus Christ.
We felt our human life could be of no importance to you;
but you have shown its value by appearing among us as a
man.
We are aware of the gulf between us and you; but you have
bridged it with love.

God, we greet your coming in Jesus Christ our Lord!

Christmas

1

Heavenly Father,
We give you praise for the ordinariness of Christmas –
    that the day comes the same as any other day.
We give you praise that there is no sign in the heavens, and no
    bright star but the light of your presence in the ordinary birth of
    the child.
We give you praise that unobtrusively you are in the centre of
    human affairs, involved in the struggle of life, and sharing human
    experience.
We give you praise that out of compassion you take our part, and
    open to us a new way of life. We pray that this day we shall be
    able to see its true glory.
Through Jesus Christ, our Lord.

2

A Meditation

Father, our complex industrial society looks for a word from you,
    and finds this simple pastoral scene of shepherds and a stable.
    Show your Church whether it's any good our going on telling the
    world this particular story.
We love it, of course. We've loved it since the Church first told it to
    us, when we were children. But it hasn't particularly helped us to
    grow up in wisdom as fast as we grew up in stature.
We thank you for the nostalgia we feel when we hear the Christmas
    story: but please, our Father, don't let us enjoy the nostalgia too
    much, in case it encourages us to let our whole religion be an
    anachronism – something that belongs to a different time in our

lives from the time we're now living in, so that we have to waste precious time thinking how to bring it back into the present again. Teach us that your Son is here, not there. Remind us that the gospel is in the fact of Christ, not in his setting; and that the story about his birth does not add up to very much without the story of his claims, his deeds, his death, and his disciples.

Father, you have brought each of us here together on the strength of some vision of your glory already seen; and in this we are not so unlike the shepherds. Help us, then, so to approach Bethlehem that our vision may be verified for us, as theirs was for them. May we, too, become part of the story of Christ's life. For his sake.

Lent

Lord God, Father, Son and Holy Spirit,
as we remember the temptation, suffering and death of Jesus Christ
help us to take up the cross and follow him.

Lord God, save us
  from the hurt pride that leads to anger
  so that we nurse our grudges and resentments
  and refuse to love and forgive.
By the power of the Holy Spirit
  help us to do as Jesus did –
    love our enemies
    pray for our persecutors
    and forgive others the wrongs they have done.
      In his name we ask it.

Lord God, save us
  from the self-centredness that makes us blind to the needs of
    others
  because we begrudge the time and money and effort
  we might have to spend in helping them.
By the power of the Holy Spirit
  help us to live as Jesus lived –
    always ready to listen
    never too tired to help
    always living not for ourselves
    but for you and for other men.
      In his name we ask it.

Lord God, save us
  from the selfishness that turns us in on ourselves
  so that we put ourselves first
  and push other people out of our way.
By the power of the Holy Spirit
  help us to do as Jesus did –
    leave self behind
    and take up the cross.
      In his name we ask it.

Now to you, our God,
Father, Son and Holy Spirit,
we give all honour and praise
for ever and ever.

2

As the time approached when Jesus was to be taken up to heaven,
he set his face resolutely towards Jerusalem.

(Luke 9.51 NEB, adapted)

Peter said: 'I am ready to go with you to prison and death.'
Jesus said: 'I tell you, Peter, the cock will not crow tonight until
you have three times over denied that you know me.'

(Luke 22.33-34 NEB, adapted)

Lord Jesus, we have come together to worship you because we want
  to be your disciples. We want to be resolute as you were when
  you set your face towards Jerusalem.

But we know that our resolution has been more like Peter's, when
  he denied that he knew you. And we have had far less justification
  than he. We know that we are constantly in need of your forgiveness and your help if we are to become your disciples.

So we come trusting that just as you did not wash your hands of Peter because he denied you, but called him to feed your sheep, so you are ready to forgive and help us. Feed us, we pray, in this worship, and equip us with all that we need to be your ministers in the world.

3

'He set his face resolutely towards Jerusalem.'

(Luke 9.51 NEB)

Heavenly Father,
Love is vulnerable –
   this we learn from your Son as he approaches the hostile city,
      cost what it may;
   this we learn from you, as down the repetitive years you make
      your approach to man, and feel the callous hurt of human pride.

Make us sensitive to your coming, that we may understand that you
   lay yourself open to our spite.
Give us to repent, and to live carefully, that we add no more to your
   grief.

Through Jesus Christ, our Lord.

Palm Sunday

Lord Jesus Christ

When you entered Jerusalem, the people spread a carpet of palm branches before you, and shouted, 'Blessings on him who comes in the name of the Lord'.
Lord Jesus, we want to join them in their welcome and their praise.

When you were handed over to the authorities, flogged and put to death, you still seemed more like a king than a criminal.
Lord Jesus, even your cross looks like a throne: always and everywhere you are in control.

When the people's praises turned to jeering and they shouted, 'Crucify!', you prayed for their forgiveness.
Lord Jesus, we know that we are the same sort of people as those who jeered at you then: we too need your forgiveness.

When you were raised from the tomb, men were brought to see in your living and your dying the surpassing love of God.
Lord Jesus, nothing in all creation can separate us from the love of God which we meet in you.

Praise and honour, glory and might, be to him who sits on the throne and to the Lamb, for ever and ever.

2

(*Versicle*: Master, we hear your call:
Response: Lord Jesus, help us to follow.)

Jesus said: 'Whoever among you wants to be great must become the servant of all. For the Son of Man himself has not come to be served but to serve, and to give his life to set many others free.'
  Master, we hear your call:
  People: Lord Jesus, help us to follow.

Jesus said: 'Unless you change your whole outlook and become like little children you will never enter the kingdom of heaven.'
  Master, we hear your call:
  People: Lord Jesus, help us to follow.

Jesus said: 'Blessed are the poor in spirit, for theirs is the kingdom of heaven. Blessed are the meek, for they shall inherit the earth.'
  Master, we hear your call:
  People: Lord Jesus, help us to follow.

Jesus said: 'You must love your enemies, and do good without expecting any return and without giving up hope of anyone: so will you be sons of the Most High, because he himself is kind to the ungrateful and wicked. Be compassionate, as your Father is compassionate.'
  Master, we hear your call:
  People: Lord Jesus, help us to follow.

Jesus said: 'This is my Father's glory, that you may bear fruit in plenty and so be my disciples. He who dwells in me, as I dwell in him, bears much fruit; for apart from me you can do nothing.'
  Master, we hear your call:
  People: Lord Jesus, help us to follow.

Jesus said: 'There is no greater love than this, that a man should lay down his life for his friends. This is my commandment; love one another, as I have loved you.'

Master, we hear your call:

People: Lord Jesus, help us to follow.

Jesus said: 'All power in heaven and on earth has been given to me. You, then, are to go and make disciples of all the nations and baptize them in the name of the Father and of the Son and of the Holy Spirit. Teach them to observe all that I have commanded you. And remember, I am with you always, even to the end of the world.'

Master, we hear your call:

People: Lord Jesus, help us to follow.

(*Scripture references for the respective sections are as follows: Mark 10.43 Phillips; Matthew 18.3 Phillips; Matthew 5.3, 5 RSV; Luke 6.35 NEB, with margin; John 15.8, 5 NEB; John 15.13, 12 NEB; and Matthew 28.18 Phillips.*)

Christ's Passion and Death

1

Washing the Disciples' Feet

Lord Jesus

Although you were their leader, you washed your disciples' feet,
dressing and acting as their servant. Make us servants to each
other. Rid us of pride and vain ambition. And give us true
humility, both to serve others and to be served by you.

2

Remembering Gethsemane

Lord Jesus, help us to know that the weight of our sins was the
cause of your pain, and that the cup which you feared was our
distance from God. Then let us weep not for you but for ourselves,
yet rejoice that your love has reached us.

3

Lord Jesus, like your disciples, we have been loud in our protesta-
tions of loyalty to you, and yet we have turned out to be disloyal.
You trod the way of love without flinching: we hesitate to tread
it at all. We have been afraid of the pain and suffering which love
brings.

But it has done us no good to follow the easy way, for it has made us
less than the men and women we could have been. So we must
follow your way, even though it is hard, for it is the way to true
life.

Give us the courage to stand by you in your hour of grief, and not to run away. Keep us loyal and devoted to the end, always open to the Father's will and to the needs of our fellow men, for your sake.

4

Good Friday

Heavenly Father

We find the story of this day unbearable. It is bad enough that Jesus of Nazareth should have been put to death on a cross, but we realize that this was not so much the act of specially wicked men as the awful result of ordinary human attitudes. To our horror we see where all human spite finds its target, and we admit our share in this guilt of humanity which would drive us to utter despair.

This day's story is unbearable indeed – to all except yourself. At this we marvel, that your love is great enough to take the monotonous hurt of all human wrongs. Guilty, yet grateful, at the foot of the cross we receive your forgiveness, and pray that you will enable us to live in dependence on your love.

Through Jesus Christ, our Lord.

5

We feel ashamed, God, as we consider the sufferings of Jesus, for we know that he suffered because he made himself open to others in love, and we know how miserably we fail to do that. We admit that sometimes we even resent Jesus, for he is a standing reminder to us that our lives are lacking in love. We have been afraid to give ourselves to other people for fear of the suffering it might involve. We have shut ourselves up, risking nothing in case we lose all, fearful of being hurt. And the quality of Jesus' love and the suffering that he accepted put us to shame.

Forgive our refusal to accept suffering as part of love. Stop us from
wanting to be safe at all costs. Give us the courage to open ourselves in love to others, and to be willing to expose ourselves to
the risk of suffering for Jesus' sake.

6

*On Good Friday, at a communion service, these words may be used as
a call to worship or opening meditation.*

Brothers and sisters in Christ

On the first Good Friday
the disciples went from the supper-table to the cross
   bewildered, anxious and afraid;
   to the shock of death and grief;
   to the shattering of all their hopes.
Today, by the grace of God,
we go from the cross to the table
   not in bewilderment – but in wonder;
   not in fear – but in joy;
   not anxious – but at peace.

At the cross, our Lord who dies for us
demands of us
   the death of all that is wrong in us,
   the shattering of selfish hopes.
At the table, our Lord who lives with us
gives to us
   the life that lifts us up from death,
   the hope that rests on the love of God.

Thanks be to God!

Easter

1

Jesus is risen from the dead – the very first to rise of all who sleep
the sleep of death.
> He died once – there and then.
> He lives for ever – here and now.

℟ God our Father, how glad you make us! What light and hope you
give us!
There is nothing that can come between us and your love.
> Not even our sins, for in Jesus you have forgiven everyone who
> is sorry for the evil he has done.
> Not even illness and danger and death, for in Jesus you have
> battled with these and won a great victory.
All thanks to you, then, our God, for the victory you are passing on
to us through our Lord Jesus Christ.

22|4|73. **2**
(Especially when children are present)

Dear Father,
This is the best day of the whole year –
> the best day of all time.
For on Easter Day we find that Jesus, who was dead, is alive again:
> and in the tokens of bread and wine we find his promise that those
> also who put their trust in him shall not be swept away by death,
> but shall have eternal life.

On this day of light and gladness, help us to put darkness out of our
lives.

Make us willing and able to change our old ways of thinking and
speaking and doing into Easter ways: so that how we behave may
bear out what we believe, and so that Christ's new creation may
become in us not just a hope but a fact.
Through the same Jesus Christ our Lord, who lives and reigns with
you, our Father, and the Holy Spirit, one God for ever and ever.

3

The Lord is risen!
He is risen indeed!
Alleluia!

Lord Jesus, we greet you, risen from the dead.
We thought that your way of love was a dead end, leading only to
a cross:
now we see that it is the way to life.
We thought that your whole life was wasted:
now we know that it was gloriously worthwhile.
We thought that your suffering was pointless:
now we can see God's purpose in it.
We thought that death was the end of you:
now we know that your life was too great to be ended by death.
Lord Jesus, we adore you, risen from the dead.

4

Father,
Life begins again today.
Jesus lives again today.

He lives for ever with you, beyond the limitations of human life,
Lord of time and space.
– We praise you.
He lives for ever with us, bringing your life into our life,
Lord of here and now.
– We praise you.

Father,
As we welcome the good news of his life with you –
    his unlimited power and love –
May we know the effects of his life with us:
    compassion, kindness, patience,
    the love that binds us together,
    the courage to forgive and be forgiven.

Father,
Since life begins again today
Help us to make a new beginning
with Jesus our Lord.

(*Based on Col. 3.1, 12* NEB)

5

Let us worship the God and Father of our Lord Jesus Christ:
    and because in his mercy he has given us new birth into a
        living hope by the resurrection of Jesus from the dead;
    because he has brought us into an inheritance that nothing
        can destroy or spoil or wither;
    because this is cause for great joy, a joy too great for words;
        let us silently adore him.

(*A silence*)

Praise without limit, glory without end, be yours everlastingly,
    God and Father of our Lord Jesus Christ.

And let us readily acknowledge our need of forgiveness.
    Lord Jesus Christ, forgive us our slowness in believing and our
    difficulties in understanding the mystery of Easter. From where
    you are now with the Father, accept our faith and help us where
    faith falls short. And since you showed yourself alive to those who
    looked for you in a tomb, forgive us the way we still think of you
    locked in the past. Help us to grasp that you are permanently
    risen; so that remembering you as you were we may worship you
    as you are.

6

Lord God, it is proper and good for us always and everywhere to give you thanks.

But today more than ever we give you the utmost thanks, for your goodness defying description which raised Jesus Christ from the dead.

For the stamp of approval you set on his life,
> for reviving men's trust in your goodness and power, we praise you.

Help us to see the place of the resurrection in the full sweep of your purpose.

Help us to realize that Jesus is permanently risen.

Help us to value the promise he gave his disciples, that he died on purpose to prepare a place for us, to pave the way for the Holy Spirit's work among us.

We pray for the earth on which he died and was raised.

Give the Church clarity and courage in spreading the news Jesus gave about you.

Give us more imagination to see and more generosity to meet the needs of those who find it hard to trust you.

And since so much of our life is affected by the decisions of a few, make them equal to the temptations and demands of their power.

Lord God,
> What you have done is great and astounding.
> The way you have taken is just and true.
> Who can revere you enough or do homage too much?

Lord Christ,
> You are the glorious king.
> You are the Son of the Father uniquely.
> Now you have freed us by your death,
>> keep us part of your people for ever.

7

'He has been raised from the dead and is going on before you into Galilee; there you will see him.'

(Matt. 28.7 NEB)

Heavenly Father,

We praise you that Christ has borne in himself the brunt of all the evil of the world to outlive it – that he is way ahead on the far frontiers of human anxiety offering to people at their wits' end the relevant help of his presence.

Give us the desire to follow him into the challenging places of life, knowing that we shall find him there ahead of us. Help us to keep up with our Lord.

8

Lord Jesus Christ,

As we know that your cross was once lifted in public derision, help us to picture your high exaltation over everything, everywhere, always; and to rejoice that our hearts can be lifted and drawn to you now, so that we dwell in you and you in us: till you bring us to the place you have gone to prepare for us.

Ascension

1

Ascended Lord Jesus, you are the pioneer of our salvation,
the leader who delivers us.

You have found a way through life's maze
and won through to the centre of things.
You have blazed a trail through all the confusing tangles of life
and opened up a path for us.
You were the first to struggle through to perfection.
We adore you.

Lead us along the path to God
and bring us through all our struggles
to the perfection you have achieved.

Ascended Lord Jesus, our leader, pioneer of salvation,
we adore you!

2

Ascended Lord Jesus, we adore you!

Once you lived a human life subject to the limitations of time:
now you are the same yesterday, today and for ever.
Once you were limited to one particular place:
now you are present wherever men turn to vou.
Once only those who met you face to face knew you:
now your divine love extends through all the world.

Jesus, ascended Lord of time and space,
love as wide as life,
we adore you!

Whitsun

Jesus said:

> 'I will not leave you bereaved. I will ask the Father and he will give you another – who will be with you for ever. He will call to mind all that I have told you; everything he makes known to you he will draw from what is mine. It is to your good that I am leaving you. For if I go I will send him to you.'
>
> (John 14-15, selected verses)

Let us adore the Holy Spirit, who was there at creation sweeping the emptiness and bringing the universe from God's will to birth.
Let us adore the Holy Spirit, who brought about the greater creation, when the Word was made flesh for us in Jesus.
Let us adore the Holy Spirit, who came to disciples like fire and a wind, so that the power in their lives was then God's power.

And let us pray to the Holy Spirit.
Holy Spirit,

> As we are together in one place, believing in God's love because of Jesus, and needing again the resources to live our lives well: make us sensitive to your presence within us; give us the skill to detect your activity in the world around us; help us to attempt what we know to be good, sure of your power at hand to help us: and bring us the joy of communion with God, as by your help we say: Our Father . . .

2

Spirit of God, powerful and unpredictable as the wind.

You came upon the followers of Jesus on the first Whitsunday and
swept them off their feet, so that they found themselves doing
what they thought they never had it in them to do.
It is you who through all ages have fired men with enthusiasm to
go about telling the good news of Jesus and serving other people
for his sake.

Spirit of God, powerful and unpredictable as the wind,
come upon us as we worship and become the driving force of
our lives.

Trinity

1

God the Father, God beyond us, we adore you.
  You are the depth of all that is.
  You are the ground of our being.
  We can never grasp you, yet you grasp us;
    the universe speaks of you to us, and your love comes to us
    through Jesus.

God the Son, God beside us, we adore you.
  You are the perfection of humanity.
  You have shown us what human life should be like.
  In you we see divine love and human greatness combined.

God the Spirit, God around us, we adore you.
  You draw us to Jesus and the Father.
  You are the power within us.
  You give us abundant life and can make us the men and women
    we are meant to be.

Father, Son, and Spirit;
God, beyond, beside and around us;
We adore you.

2

We praise and adore you, God our Father.
  You are the maker of everything,
    and because of your will
    things came to be and continue in being.

We praise and adore you, Jesus Christ.
   You are the Word made flesh,
      and because of your life
      we both know the Father and trust his love.
We praise and adore you, Holy Spirit.
   You are the Father's gift to men,
      and because of your ceaseless activity
      nothing is cut off from God.
With the whole Church on earth and in heaven we praise and adore
   you,
      for the wonder of your power,
      the marvel of your mercy,
      and the patience of your purpose for mankind.

All Saints

Living God, give us grace to take to heart your living word.
As nothing can divide us from your love in Christ Jesus, so grant
that nothing may divide your people from one another.

Shake us out of our contentment with a divided Church.
In our thanksgiving for the saints in heaven, deliver us from
imagining them as all our sort of people.
And in our dealings with our fellow Christians on earth, show us
how to be true to our consciences without being untrue to the
law of love.

Father, we pray that each of us may take home today a greater
awareness of your vast and comprehensive purpose – big enough
to include the countless hosts of faithful men and women who
have already lived, those who are alive today, and those who are
yet unborn.
Help us to be sure that although so many are included within your
love, not one is nameless, or confused by you with another.
And let this awareness and this assurance give us a new sense of
occasion about our daily life and work, since we know that in the
Lord our labour cannot be lost.

We have prayed for the unity of the Church on earth, and for the
knowledge of our unity with the Church in heaven.
We pray now for the unity of all mankind, and for your merciful
help wherever there is strife and destruction, cruelty and oppres-
sion.
Since you are the author of human rights, let it be seen that your
Spirit champions the cause of equality and brotherhood no matter
where.

Since you have made every race of men in your image, stop us from using the Bible to bolster our prejudice and disdain.
May men's hopes for the world be fulfilled as they serve you, till the whole world becomes your place, as you always intended.

Through Jesus Christ our Lord.

APPENDIX
The Lord's Prayer

The Lord's Prayer

Father in heaven,
May your name be honoured,
Your kingdom come,
Your will be done on earth as in heaven.
Give us each day our daily bread.
Forgive us the wrong we have done
   as we forgive others the wrong they have done to us.
And do not bring us to the test,
But save us from evil.
For yours is the kingdom and the power and the glory for ever. Amen

Paraphrases

I

Our Father in heaven,
May we honour here on earth
   Every sign of your presence,[1]
   Every act of your rule,
   Every item of your plan,
As it stands in heaven.
Give us what we need each day, a day at a time:
And forgive us our offences
   in the same measure as we forgive those who have wronged us.
Do not bring us to a testing which is beyond our power to withstand.
For you have the power, and the authority,
And the glory is for ever yours.

   [1] Taking God's 'name' to mean his revelation of himself to men.

2

God, our Father,
Make a name for yourself among men.
May everyone acknowledge and obey you.
May your purpose be achieved on earth as in heaven.
Give us today the food we need;
And forgive us the wrong we have done
   as we have already forgiven those who have wronged us.
Don't bring us to breaking-point,[1]
But lead us out of harm's way.
For you are the one who can do all this;
Nothing will ever overpower you;
The highest honour is yours always.

3

Father in heaven,
May everything praise you.
Rule as you wish.
Achieve what you want on earth – as in heaven.
Give us each day what we need:
And forgive us the wrong we have done
As we forgive those who have wronged us.
And guide us away from temptation:
Release us from evil.
For you are our mighty and glorious king
And always will be.

[1] Cf. the version in Hooper and Marvin's play, *A Man Dies*: 'Don't test us past our breaking-point.'

4

Heavenly Father, you alone are God.
May your kingdom come, and your will be done
   on earth as it is in heaven.
Please give us today what you think we need:
Forgive us the wrong things that we do,
   and may we be ready to forgive others.
Spare us from the testing which is beyond our strength;
   and break evil's hold upon us.
For yours is the kingdom whose days are not numbered,
Yours the power which shall not end,
Yours the glory which shall never fade.